START

The who-wants-to-be-perfect-anyway approach

WITH

to experiencing more fulfilling relationships

YOU

REBECCA MILLER

For Anike!

With love,

Becca xx

Praise

'Rebecca is a hugely valuable part of the well-being team here at Lifehouse. Her knowledge, skills, humour and enthusiasm make her very popular both with regular and new guests. Rebecca always demonstrates empathy and warmth which makes people instantly feel at ease with her. Her insight and compassion makes clients feel they can share anything without being judged and we regularly receive fabulous feedback as to the results she creates. In her book, *Start With You*, Rebecca has given a glimpse of what it is like to work with her in real life; her knowledge and empathy shine through. By using personal anecdotes Rebecca demonstrates her extensive insight, skill and knowledge as a coach through making the questions and theories she raises both accessible and relevant to the reader. This book will make you smile and reassure you that you are not alone and that you too can learn to accept yourself for who you are and then create more of what you want in your relationships and life.'

SUE DAVIS, WELL-BEING DIRECTOR AT LIFEHOUSE SPA AND HOTEL

'Rebecca's book is the perfect distillation of everything that she brings to her practice. It's her wonderful, warm, down to earth personality and professional understanding all in one.'

BONNIE FRIEND, WRITER AND EDITOR

'Rebecca Miller's, *Starting With You* is an elegant tapestry of authenticity, delightful humour and powerful awakenings. This book is equally entertaining and filled with invitations to use our own experiences to raise your awareness about your relationships. I highly recommend to RSVP to these invitations and create relationships you would love!'

BETH WOLFE, LIFE MASTERY COACH.

'*Start With You* is an enlightening and remarkably relatable approach to the creation of fulfilling relationships in our lives. By first minding our own perspective and power in how we connect with ourselves and others, Rebecca skilfully demonstrates how to develop understanding and growth in the most crucial relational issues we encounter. The combination of both personal revelations and professional expertise will leave readers with the kind of insight and know-how that might normally require years of training and consulting with an advanced relationship coach.'

JEREMY FUHS, LIFE COACH

'Really refreshing take on how your own needs impact your relationships. A must read for understanding yourself better.'

IVAN FAES, BREAKTHROUGH AND PERFORMANCE COACH

'An incredibly honest and readable book; made me laugh out loud as I could recognise myself on virtually every page! I love the combination of personal anecdotes with professional insight.'

LIZ CARRIGHAN, EXECUTIVE COACH AND TRAINER

RETHINK PRESS

First published in Great Britain 2017
by Rethink Press (www.rethinkpress.com)

© Copyright Rebecca Miller

For Mum and Dad, in loving memory

Contents

Foreword   1

Introduction   5

1. The Fundamentals Of Starting With You   19

2. Hello, Have We Met Before?   37

3. Understanding The Imposter Syndrome   51

4. The Ex-Files And How To Deal With Them   67

5. Spotting The Toxic Relationship   85

6. Needs Versus Wants   99

7. Trusting Your Instincts In A Relationship   115

8. Calling Mr Right   131

9. When Our Most Important Relationship
    Is With Our Pet   149

10. Six Needs And Getting The Right Ingredients   163

    Resources   175

    Acknowledgements   181

    The Author   183

Foreword

Aren't you simply fed up with the need to be perfect?

The model student, the helpful child, the doting partner, the superhero parent, the exemplary employee...?

Compounding the exhaustion of people pleasing are the self-sabotaging thoughts that constantly remind you that you are not good enough. Not to mention the destructive behavioural habits that keep us feeling damaged, separate and alone.

The push to be perfect, internally and externally, is such a waste of this one precious life.

The good news is, the beliefs and behaviours that have you feeling unworthy, unfulfilled and unlovable are just habits. They can be changed.

You have the power to choose a different way of doing life and I just love the way Rebecca, in a way that is so beautiful and relatable, shares tools to help you identify what needs to change in your life and how to make it happen.

There is a massive misperception in our society that if we dare to think about ourselves and put ourselves first the people we love most are going to suffer.

It's a lie.

The truth is, when we can learn to love ourselves enough to put ourselves first, the people we cherish will get the best of us. Relationships in all areas of our life can thrive when we dare to dig deep into the truth of who we are and discover that we are worthy of honouring the callings of our soul.

Self-Love requires self responsibility. No-one but you can change your life. No-one but you can put an end to sabotaging the things you want most in life, and for the majority of people that boils down to peace, happiness and a sense that they are loved and able to love.

You are not damaged. You are not unworthy. You are not less than anyone else.

You are a beautiful spirit. You are perfect. You are pure love.

Your assignment is to remember who you are, heal anything that is blocking you to being that glorious creature, and get out in the world, shine your light and be of massive contribution to this planet.

Rebecca is so qualified to help you on your journey back home to yourself. Sure, she has oodles of qualifications and extensive experience as a coach. More than that, she has taken responsibility for her life and done the deep and often confronting work to investigate any patterns in her life that have had her be anything less than her true self. She then vulnerably and humorously shares her experiences in this book to prove to you that change is possible. That level of authenticity and honesty is rare. It's also invaluable to you if you want to change because she reassures you that you are not alone and that you can create any life and any feeling that you desire.

You get one shot at this beautiful life.
I dare you to follow Rebecca's lead and make it mighty!

Katie Phillips
Author of *The Self-Love Affair – A Woman's Guide To A Daring And Mighty Life*, www.daringandmighty.com

Introduction

'But you're a Life Coach, aren't you? I thought you were supposed to be good at communicating and dealing with people.'

And that was the final nail in the coffin of an argument I'd been having with a friend from drama group whom I had just blasted for not being ready when I came to pick him up.

Mikey was part of a small crowd I was driving to a rehearsal, and somehow communication wires had got crossed and he wasn't waiting outside when I arrived. When I called him, he nonchalantly informed me that as he hadn't known when exactly I would be arriving, he hadn't seen the point in moving from his house.

All reasonable so far. Unfortunately, we were on a tight schedule so, tired and irritable, I chose not to see it that way. Instead, I proceeded to treat him to a caustic tirade at his inconsideration and selfishness.

Mikey's response was very calm. He informed me that he absolutely would not tolerate being spoken to like that.

You would think that being a Life Coach of reasonable intelligence and many years of experience, I would have honoured the sense in that remark and apologised. But, no.

'Well, forgive me, but I also happen to be a human being. Next time you are running your workshop on how to be perfect, do let me know and I'll sign up,' was my ever so adult response.

Ouch!

After flouncing off in true drama queen style, I burst into tears. Finally, I found Mikey to apologise. He was very gracious, but pointed out that if he allowed himself to be treated like that, it would not be fair to himself, or anyone else. Spoken exactly as I would encourage a client to feel and respond, and a wonderful example of the concept of starting with you and owning your own emotions.

Double ouch.

So how and why did I allow myself to respond like that? I agonised about this for a few days, asking friends if I was an angry, confrontational person with a mean line in sarcasm when pushed. The universal response was no. However, some friends did go on to point out that I wasn't afraid to confront people or issues when need be, and my quick temper was sometimes in evidence.

Then one close friend asked the killer question. While I was indulging in my tirade against Mikey, had I enjoyed it?

Oh dear. The truth is yes, I had to a certain extent. Don't get me wrong, I don't like deliberately causing hurt or offence, but I would be lying if I said I hadn't enjoyed the freedom of letting rip and allowing the diva side of me out for a change.

Then I looked at it from a coaching perspective. Why had a seemingly innocuous incident triggered such dramatic reactions in me?

As a student of Dr Eric Berne's 'Transactional Analysis', I rationalised my response. Transactional Analysis allows us to understand our triggers and responses to people based on our early life. How did we feel we had to react to others in order to survive? This in later life leads us to enter unconsciously into either parent, adult or child state, and does not always lead to great outcomes, as my example demonstrates.

Mikey's comment, expressed in an adult and mature way, really got me thinking. He was absolutely right. If he were to accept being treated unfairly or harshly by others, what would that say about how he regarded himself?

Which Transactional Analysis state had I been in with Mikey? Parent mode initially. I was being judgmental and felt the need to point out the error of his ways, as I saw them, and what he 'should' be doing or feeling in order to match my views. Mikey stayed entirely adult throughout, calmly pointing out that such behaviour was unacceptable to him, until the 'But aren't you a Life Coach?' comment. Then he too entered the parent mode, which triggered me to become a rebellious child and blast him.

In the cold light of day, I returned to adult and apologised, explaining my behaviour as the result of feeling stressed and tired without offering this as an excuse.

Ultimately, I questioned where my need to be seen as perfect, both as a coach and a person, actually came from. I asked myself the following:

♡ What was it that triggered me to respond like this, and how much of it is a pattern in my relationships?

♡ What excuses had I been creating in order to feel OK about responding like this?

♡ What needs was I meeting and not meeting by striving for an image of perfection?

♡ How often was I in adult mode *inside* as opposed to how I chose to present myself and respond on the outside?

♡ What did I need to take ownership of and what did I really want?

♡ How could I use my own experiences and understanding to provide a context for others to raise this awareness for themselves?

And then came two realisations that I heartily encourage with my clients: none of us is perfect, and we all have control over what we choose to believe, feel and think, and how we behave. However, developing this awareness requires a strong willingness to take ownership and create the necessary changes to feel more fulfilled in our relationships.

'God grant me the serenity to accept the things I cannot change, the courage to change the things I can, and the wisdom to know the difference.'

REINHOLD NIEBUHR

In the past, I found it difficult to articulate a coherent answer to questions such as:

♡ How do you help people exactly?

♡ What is so different about you?

♡ What theory and approach do you use?

♡ What's the difference between coaching and giving advice or counselling?

♡ Are all your relationships perfect?

The standard responses explain the differences between coaching and counselling, and how coaching works with the client to move them forwards from a new point of awareness rather than staying focused on the past. And no, I never once said that my relationships are all perfect, often referring to some pretty major mistakes to illustrate how I learnt what makes them imperfect. To trusted friends and colleagues, I even admitted that the more I learnt about all things relating to human behaviour and psychology, the more confused I got. The kind of coach I wanted to be became all the more difficult to decide as my butterfly mind loved learning new things and making connections, dipping into the smorgasbord of authors, theories and approaches extolled by highly regarded experts in the field.

I did, however, know that I wanted to focus on relationships as I felt, being somewhat long in the tooth, I might actually have something to offer. Not because I had worked out the perfect system or answer, or indeed had the ultimate relationship, but because my experiences and studies allowed me to create genuine empathy with my clients. I could relate to most of the key patterns and issues they were facing in their relationships.

My turning point in recognising my own patterns and triggers within my relationships was when I came across the work of Tony Robbins. Robbins is truly a master in his field who has had phenomenal success. He developed his approach by taking the best and most applicable psychology and therapy theories and practices to create positive change. I experienced a surge of 'Aha!' moments as Robbins's approach helped me clarify everything else I had studied.

Robbins's work is based on the premise that we all have six needs: Certainty, Variety, Significance, Love and Connection, Growth and Contribution. We then prioritise and meet those needs in different ways that can have both a positive and negative impact on our lives and relationships. The quality of my experiences lay in understanding these six needs and recognising the thoughts, rules and behaviours I had created around them.

This provided me with the insight to recognise how I had developed patterns of feeling, thinking, responding and behaving, leading me to acknowledge the mistakes I had made in the past so I could spot the danger signs in new relationships. Then I would be able to make different choices as to how to respond and relate to them. And, even better, I could celebrate being different and embrace all of my quirks and flaws without feeling that I had to be perfect.

So why am I writing this book if all that wonderful stuff is already out there? While we may all have the same kinds of experiences, knowledge and skills, how we interpret and respond to them is unique to each individual. No matter how many books I read, and no matter how great the content, some have resonated with me more than others.

Life is full of twists, turns and dramas, most of which we create for ourselves. If we were to get it right all of the time, life and relationships would be very dull. And having gone through many dramas and traumas in my own life, I am far more in favour of creating variety and fun through positive means than the toxic patterns I found myself repeating by choosing the wrong type again and again.

From childhood, as with so many people, I developed the belief that I wasn't good enough or loveable enough unless I met specific rules and expectations set by other influential people in my life. My need to feel safe and secure led me to be controlling, continually seeking ways to belong in all the wrong places and willingly entering toxic relationships on a regular basis, even though I knew they weren't going to make me happy. I developed a great 'persona' so people thought I was confident and fabulous, completely unaware that I was living every day with the belief that 'if they really knew me, they would run a mile'. If I let my vulnerability show or displayed any kind of 'challenging' behaviours, I thought I would be vilified.

And so the loop continued. I still struggle with some of it today, but I'm a heck of a lot more aware now and have the experience to recognise the patterns and stop them by applying the tools I have learnt. I recognise the fact that I will always be a work in progress, which is a good thing as it makes my clients more able to relate to me as I come across as human. I embrace the fact that no one is perfect, but I do not use that as an excuse to continue to make poor choices, and that essentially is what this book is about. We have nowhere better to start than with ourselves.

Start With You is not about dismissing the traumas we have experienced, but about truly owning our emotions and behaviours and raising our awareness as to the choices we have made as a result of those traumas. However, we may have lots of blocks that are difficult to shift.

I have found that by using stories and 'scripts' from my own experiences to create a relative context for clients and friends, I can help them understand their own patterns, rules and needs, identifying that how they choose to meet them defines the quality of their relationships with both themselves and others. This then makes the theories, books, strategies and approaches I recommend far more relevant. Comments such as: 'Oh my God, I actually have said that!' or 'That is exactly what it felt like' or 'Did you know my mother/partner/ boss/friend as you have just described them to a tee?' or even 'Were you in the room with us?' have not been uncommon. And no, I was not in the room. I am not that kind of girl.

I do not want to give a condensed version of all the theories already out there or offer another 'how to' book. I also do not want to suggest that this book will take the place of the excellent therapies, theories and approaches that I will refer to. So what *will* this book give you?

Well, through anecdotes and stories about my own experiences, I want to offer readers the opportunity to access and understand the concepts of the '6 Human Needs' and 'Transactional Analysis'. By narrating my stories in the context of the insights and learning I have gained then asking questions, I will invite readers to recognise some of the common themes and issues we all experience in our relationships, and demonstrate that when we raise our awareness, we can change our intent and what we choose to do. Each chapter will provide a contextual story to explore themes such as feeling like an imposter, continually choosing the 'wrong type', always trying to 'fix' our partners, believing the dream rather than the reality, recognising and escaping from toxic relationships, coping with the ex, understanding the difference between being selfish and selfless, and when we use pets as substitutes for a real relationship. This will lead on to questions centred around the *Start With You* approach.

You may find it useful to jot down notes as you read through each chapter and then use them to access the resource suggestions or to talk through with a trusted friend as you feel appropriate.

My personal interpretation of *Start With You* is taking ownership of ourselves and our own well-being so we can be open to new possibilities and choices in how we understand ourselves and others.

Yourself. You are you, warts and all, and have your own experiences, thoughts and beliefs to prove it. Whatever our individual circumstances and background, we all share the same six needs and have choices in how we meet them. We may not always find it easy to acknowledge this, or even know how to change our choices, but taking ownership of our choices and emotions is the vital first step. Then we can identify what further support we may need in order to feel prepared, both physically and emotionally, to make better choices.

The stories and questions in this book aim to raise your awareness of how you can take more ownership of yourself and what you can choose to do differently.

Others. To make more healthy and fulfilling choices in our relationships, we need to think creatively and experience positive emotions that will alter our perceptions. There is a huge choice in how this can be achieved and everyone has different preferences. As long as you find a way that suits you, then you are more likely to follow through to improve your relationships.

Understanding. This is endless and unique to each individual. Understanding what possibilities are out there means being open to new ways of feeling, thinking, behaving, communicating, acting, dreaming and doing. It is great that there are so many different self-help books and techniques and strategies because it is all about personal choice. Whatever resonates with you will work for you.

'Transactional Analysis' and '6 Human Needs Psychology' are so interesting for me because they provide the opportunity to see beneath the patterns and behaviours we take for granted, opening the door for new ways of thinking and communicating. The question then becomes: 'Knowing what I know now, what can I choose to do differently?'

ONE

The Fundamentals Of Starting With You

'The best years of your life are the ones in which you
decide your problems are your own. You do not blame
them on your mother, the ecology, or the president.
You realize that you control your own destiny.'

DR ALBERT ELLIS, PSYCHOLOGIST

Such wise words, yet so many people have become conditioned to blaming others for the state of their relationships that the equally wise words of the poet Philip Larkin – 'They f*** you up, your mum and dad. They may not mean to, but they do' – are the ones they subscribe to.

'Parents, deliberately or unaware, teach their
children from birth how to behave, think, feel and
perceive. Liberation from these influences is no easy
matter, since they are deeply ingrained...'

ERIC BERNE, THE FOUNDER OF TRANSACTIONAL ANALYSIS

However, according to Epictetus, the Greek Philosopher, 'It is not what happens to you, but how you react to it that matters.'

In light of this and before we go any further, take a moment to complete the following quick exercise:

In an average week, write down all the emotions you usually experience. Next, sort them into a list of positive, negative and neutral.

How many emotions did you write down? What is the balance of positive, negative, neutral? When do you usually experience these emotions? In what circumstances and triggered by who in your life?

All of this will help with the purpose behind the rest of the chapter and book and will be expanded upon further in the resource section.

Well, now we have a bit of a dilemma. Do we choose to believe that our past defines us and that the beliefs and behaviours we develop are deeply ingrained and therefore beyond our control? Or do we choose to believe that we all have inner resources that allow us to make different decisions and take more control over responding to our own 'map of the world', as Neuro Linguistic Programming (NLP) calls it? Do we use our past as an excuse for our present situations, echoing my late father's stock response of, 'I cannae help it!' to any feedback about his behaviour and its impact? Or do we echo my incredible pal, Jeremy, who aged fifteen decided, 'This is not who I want to be. I am going to choose a different role model for myself'? Jeremy wasn't judging his parents; he was just exercising his choice to think and behave differently, actively seeking out people who reflected the values and behaviours he wanted to create in his own life.

In my experience, both personally and as a coach, the themes of not feeling good enough, loveable enough, committed enough, responsible enough are equally common among those who have suffered difficult childhoods and those who come from loving and stable backgrounds. Going back to the theory of Epictetus, it is our response that governs our experience, not the experience itself, and this can show up as different behaviour triggers and beliefs, even between siblings who shared the same childhood experience.

I have had many 'coaching' conversations with my older brother. We obviously shared similar childhood experiences which left both of us with self-confidence and fear of rejection issues, the difference being in how these manifested themselves. Both of us, at various points displayed the appeasing, amenable child while, at other times, expressed ourselves more rebelliously. This developed some habits of communication that didn't best serve us as adults till we both reconciled ourselves to accepting the past and became more understanding of the circumstances and more compassionate, both to ourselves and others.

This also meant being more accepting of the time period we grew up in and that how we were viewed by others also had an impact. For example, the adults around us were more allowing of how Steve, as a boy, reacted than of me, something he and I often laugh about today though it took a while for us to reconcile this.

But why was this? What were the rules that governed how each of us were regarded or treated? How does this impact on what rules we then create for ourselves in terms of the habits of response we develop and what we have learnt to do to prioritise our needs in terms of feeling love and acceptance?

Even if we raise our self-awareness of our flaws and logically deal with whatever issues come from our past, which in theory should mean we can make different choices and have better relationships, we still get triggered by certain situations and people that lead us to think and behave in limiting ways, judging ourselves and others as not being perfect enough.

For me, starting with you comes down to a willingness to recognise and understand the patterns we can identify for ourselves in our relationships as adults. Only then can we develop the wisdom to accept what is and isn't in our control and how to tell the difference.

So how does this play out in our experience? To use another NLP expression, 'There is no such thing as failure, only feedback'. Well, this is great if the feedback comes from the positive intention to help you learn from your mistakes and grow, but not so great if your pattern is to seek out people who constantly feedback that you are wrong, selfish, useless, etc. However, if we are willing to look at the patterns within our relationships and take ownership of what is driving us to choose certain types of relationships, then *all* feedback is useful and powerful as it helps us recognise the patterns we are creating and how this is making us consistently feel. Then we can have more understanding of the intent behind our choices, and the choices made by others. Understanding alone doesn't make for different choices, but it does start us on the path to getting support to clear our limiting beliefs so we can develop a healthier relationship with ourselves, becoming OK with not being perfect in our relationships, and not expecting them to be perfect either.

This fits well with the theory of Transactional Analysis. Its founder, Eric Berne, stated that fundamentally, we are all OK and have the capacity to think for ourselves and decide what we want in our life, and so take responsibility for our own actions.

Taking personal responsibility first requires us to understand and recognise that we all are hard wired to seek out love and significance from those around us, according to what we learned to respond to as small children. This explains why we may more readily go into child or adult mode to reflect what we needed to do in order to survive. However, recognising how appropriate or not these responses are now as adults and what impact, both positive and negative this creates both for ourselves and those around us is key.

So, what are some of the common patterns and beliefs that come from our past experiences? And how can recognising these help us to accept what Berne is saying? Let's start with some of the limiting beliefs we take on from early traumatic experiences and examine how they may now be playing out in our current relationships.

Unresolved resentment at feeling neglected or ignored in childhood. 'I will only choose to be with someone who is guaranteed to worry the life out of my parents [rebellious child], even though I don't feel comfortable with them and they don't treat me well.'

Role modelling key people of influence in our formative years. 'I will only choose people who exhibit behaviours that remind me of those influencers. This may mean they criticise and judge me constantly, neglect me, never make me feel important, undermine me and try to control me. This may also mean I will behave like someone I considered to be a real doormat and never argue back.'

The best way to feel accepted and loved is to put others before myself. 'I will only choose people who I feel need rescuing in some way, because if they are "damaged", they will be grateful for my love and I can satisfy my need to be needed.'

Coming from a highly volatile and dramatic background. 'I will only choose someone who guarantees constant drama. I will never feel safe with them, but will become addicted to the adrenaline rush of uncertainty and will confuse their selfish and controlling nature as proof of love.'

Parents staying together for years and years, either happily or unhappily. 'I will consistently try to make each relationship "the one", refusing to give up on it even though it is clear neither of us is happy together, because that is just what you do.'

Not feeling accepted for being ourselves. 'I will choose to stay safe even though I will go mad with boredom or frustration, because experience has taught me I'm not good looking/funny/sexy/intelligent/rich enough to attract the kind of person I really want.'

Role models whose values are superior or judgmental. 'I will choose people whom I can feel superior to as a means of making myself feel significant. I will treat them badly because I can, and because it feels good to have someone still wanting to be with me no matter what I do. However, I will hate it if I choose people who do the same to me, but I may not be able to stop myself or my patterns.'

In terms of how this relates to Human Needs Psychology, recognising patterns of thoughts and behaviours in our relationships makes more sense when we see what is driving those patterns. Tony Robbins describes the six needs as Certainty, Variety, Significance, Love and Connection, Growth and Contribution. He encourages us to ask ourselves what, exactly, has to happen for each need to be met in our relationships, and how does this impact ourselves and others close to us in both positive and negative ways?

' for the love of God, will you please go somewhere other than the United Services Club, and stop getting with single mums who are newly separated and clearly aren't ready to move on.'

'I like the club. It's my comfort zone, and it's not my fault that these women aren't ready. I'm a good bloke, surely one of them will stay around long enough to see that.'

This conversation went round on a loop for several years, with me swinging between judgmental and nurturing parent in my attempt to boost my friend's confidence and get him to inject more variety into his routine. I wanted him to look for significance by building up new interests and connections so he could feel secure without the need to compare himself to others or accept anyone who gave him some attention. I am happy to report he is now in a new relationship and a more secure place with a much stronger sense of who he is.

Now he is far too lovely to have ever turned around to me and said, 'Oh really, Bec? And let's take a look at some of your choices and behaviours, shall we? You may have changed location more frequently, but last I checked, you were still beating yourself up for not being pretty or thin enough and choosing guys who needed rescuing. With your moods and demands, sometimes you can be quite hard to be around, no matter how lovely and generous you are.'

He would have had a fair point as I was the queen of using certainty as my driver to control the circumstances and behaviours of both myself and my partners in my, shall we say, *colourful* relationships past.

The more aware we are of the intent behind our own and others' behaviours, the easier it is to decide how much we are prepared to keep running the same programmes and triggers in our current relationships. By understanding how we have chosen to view our parents/significant others and the impact this has had, we can become clear on what we would rather have, even if we don't yet feel this is within our control to achieve.

SUMMARY & QUESTIONS

We all have a past, and we all have experienced trauma, even if one person's trauma may seem like a walk in the park to someone else. The fact remains we each have a unique way of interpreting and responding to our past experiences.

Key to taking back control of those experiences is accepting another NLP idea: 'Everyone, without exception and regardless of how it may appear to others, always acts with the best possible intent for themselves, using the knowledge and resources at their disposal at that time'. Now this doesn't in any way excuse behaviours and actions, but it does give us the option to step back from them and consider the impact with more compassion, both for ourselves and others.

All of us are triggered by key events and circumstances influencing the rules and beliefs we make that then shape our own values and judgments. Taking ownership doesn't mean taking responsibility for others' behaviour, but questioning our own behaviours in the light of recognising the ideas we are using to drive them.

You. Even when we accept this logically, the emotional triggers we still have may take time and consistent effort to create lasting change and for that we may need help.

What rules and values have you taken on from your early experiences? Do they fit with who you are now and the kind of relationships you want to have? For example, do you feel it is selfish to think of yourself first, or that fundamentally there is something wrong with you? Does this lead to self-sabotage behaviours?

How does this show up in your relationships? Is your pattern to be critical and judgmental as a way of keeping control and a sense of significance? Or is it to be compliant, always trying to appease and please others as a way of being accepted and loved, even if this leads to you feeling frustrated and unhappy? Or do you find yourself constantly acting the 'needy child' and creating dramas to keep a steady flow of care and attention flowing your way?

Equally, do you find yourself being negatively triggered by the needy or dramatic behaviour of others that leads you to become hyper critical of them and judgmental? Another NLP term of 'If you spot it you've got it', can also come into play here. Sometimes, we react strongly to a behaviour we dislike in others because we fear we may have some of that trait ourselves and don't want to accept it. This may be because either we may have been harshly judged for displaying it in the past or wish we could also receive some of the attention that behaviour seems to elicit.

Are you carrying around a sense of blame or shame that is keeping you from accepting yourself, and therefore making it difficult for you to feel accepted by others?

How important is it to understand the 'why' behind what you and others do in your relationship? It is important, of course, because it can raise your awareness and give you a better idea of your or others' true intent. This can lead you to be more compassionate both to yourself and others, but do not confuse this with taking on responsibility for their choices.

Own your own choices, the intent behind them and their impact. How do you feel about yourself and others, and what now lies within your control to change?

Others. 'If you were sorry then you wouldn't keep doing it, would you?' This is a quote from my mum, when she became exasperated continually doing the same thing without actually ever learning from it or changing anything. In her eyes, she felt I was simply making excuses and not bothering to think about others even when the consequences of my actions had been pointed out to me. While she had a point, it took me years to recognise that her attitude stemmed from her own lack of self-confidence.

Life had dealt her several hard knocks which manifested in her creating clear rules for how people in relationships should behave. These rules protected her from allowing people to get too close. While she could be incredibly funny, compassionate and loving at times, she made no bones about letting others know how they disappointed her if they didn't match her expectations.

The question is then, how much of what others say to you or blame you for is down to their behaviours and responses as opposed to yours? If they are being triggered by their own past or by their own beliefs as to how others should think and respond, then they may well come across as being more child or parent in their communication than adult which may then trigger similar responses in you.

I trained as a coach after she passed away, so sadly we never got to have any conversations that would have led to us feeling more accepting or forgiving of each other. This is a hard truth for many of us. If the people you have been affected by are no longer around, accept that you cannot share your insights with them or ask them to explain their intent and actions. All you can do is choose to stop blaming them. This is not to excuse them or let them off the hook, but to help you take back control of how you want to feel and be.

We all have our reasons for protecting our sense of who we are and what we feel we need to do to meet our needs, and accepting this can allow us to view others, and ourselves, with more compassion. This can then ease our process of letting go of beliefs and patterns that are stopping us from having the kind of relationships we would prefer.

You having insight into people's 'why' doesn't mean that they will stop behaving as they do. Yes, you can express how you feel, but they may not be interested in hearing it, let alone responding to it. If they continue to behave in the same way, then that is their choice. Your choice now is to consider how to respond to this. Is it better to keep doing what you have always done and feel the way you have always felt, or to value how you feel about yourself and find the support and confidence to walk away without feeling guilty?

Understanding. I absolutely agree with the many sources who say we perpetuate what we choose to focus on, whether positive or negative. So, if we are intent on blaming our past for how we are today, we will spend all our time looking for, and finding, evidence to support that belief. Equally, muttering positive mantras and 'forgiving' is not going to work either if internally we are still feeling angry, hurt, and resentful, or feel that we are entitled to behave and respond in the ways we do.

The important thing is to get up close and personal with those emotions and acknowledge them. What needs are they serving? There is always a pay-off for everything we do, even though it may not make us happy. This is where developing awareness can lead us to become more compassionate about the intent behind not only our behaviours, but also the behaviours of others.

There is a world of difference between someone who knows themselves and their flaws yet continually says, 'Well, you know what I'm like' as an excuse to not actually do anything about it, and someone who knows their flaws, accepts they will not always get it right but who is willing to consider the impact of their behaviour on others and do something about it. As Goethe says:

> *'Knowing is not enough; we must apply.*
> *Willing is not enough; we must do.'*

Therefore, to start with you, you need to find what will work for you then choose to act.

Just because I have been shaped by my past, this doesn't mean I have no control over how I shape my future.

> *'If you don't like something, change it. If you can't*
> *change it, change your attitude. Don't complain.'*
> MAYA ANGELOU

Are you going to stick with the way things have always been or do the work and find different ways to do them? Whatever you decide, it starts with you and no one else.

TWO

Hello, Have We Met Before?

How to spot the patterns in our relationship choices

'Have we met before? Well, of course we have! I'm that lovely pattern you keep repeating in relationships, despite you being adamant that you're not going to make the same mistake again. You're going to feel and act differently and prove that you have what it takes to create a healthy relationship. Oh, really?'

This has been an announcement from your advisor, Limiting Self-belief. Thank you for listening.

I can remember returning, early and broken hearted, from a teaching job in Singapore, only to have my mum shouting at me, 'Don't be so ridiculous! You're not having a nervous breakdown, you're just being self-indulgent. If you didn't keep choosing the wrong type of man, your life wouldn't be in such a mess.'

Now, this may seem a little harsh, but I have to take ownership of the fact that there was truth in what she said. In her view, the 'wrong' type meant anyone I insisted on being with, even though they had commitment issues and clearly made me unhappy. She would see me finding as many ways possible to accommodate their needs while sinking deeper into my own personal pit of despair, then had to put up with me analysing every little thing I'd done or said while I was with them, ignoring my own sense of self-worth.

And never was I the one who instigated the break-up. No matter what my friends or my mother said, I would hang on to each relationship until circumstances became so utterly awful that my partner would choose to walk away from me. Not great when I was trying to argue with my mother that this time it really was different.

When I returned from Singapore a mere shadow of my former self in every sense of the word, it was the final straw for Mum. Yet again I had chosen to be with a seemingly charming, funny, likeable guy whom everyone loved, and I was delighted that he wanted to pursue a relationship with me. Bingo! I had instant acceptance into the whole group and a sense of belonging while away from home, all the time completely ignoring the fact that he'd made it clear after two weeks that his family background meant he had a lifelong fear of commitment.

In sensible adult mode, I would have thought, *OK, fair enough. How fab that he is being honest with me. It is not because there is anything wrong with me, it is just that he realises that continuing this relationship would be a mistake as he is not willing to commit. Let's stay friends and move on.*

Did I think like this? Did I heck! Up came all my old patterns. I needed to be the one who would change his mind. I would be so damned gorgeous and wonderful that he would throw all that commitment-phobia nonsense out of the window and have a fulfilling, fabulous relationship with me. Then I would prove to everyone that I *could* have a healthy relationship, being loved and accepted for the goddess I really am. (You can probably hear the rebellious child's foot-stamping that accompanied that declaration.)

Cue a very painful year with lots of 'on again, off again' dramas. I kept going back because I had convinced myself that love conquers all. If I could just make him happy, it would all be OK. My need to be seen to make this relationship work, and feel the certainty and significance that success would bring, meant I either ignored or constantly misinterpreted his behaviour. But far from being seen to be a loving and loyal person, I was actually judged for being an idiot for putting up with it, not to mention somewhat pathetic and desperate. Not attractive traits in anyone.

How often do we cling to relationships because the thought of being seen as having 'failed' again is so soul destroying? We blind ourselves to how wrong the relationship has clearly become and destroy all our self-worth by refusing to recognise that things sometimes just don't work out.

Yet that recognition is easier said than done, even if we have friends trying to convince us to end the relationship because they can see the inevitable train wreck we will become if we don't. And did I listen to my well-meaning friends? Did I hear them telling me that the confident, bright and funny girl they had first met was no longer anywhere to be seen? Of course not. I just retreated further inside myself, beating myself up for getting it wrong yet again and reliving all my past rejections to convince myself of how useless I was in relationships.

So how does this help me now? Well, I learnt to accept that I had made what Robbins calls 'Key Decisions' in my past that meant I was running a clear pattern in my relationships. To feel loved and accepted, I must never be 'selfish' by thinking about myself and how I felt. I always had to do and say the right thing at the right time and in the right way. By prioritising my needs for certainty and significance, I constantly tried to control myself, situations and people around me, which led to unattractive behaviours from both myself and my partner.

And then came the critical comments from well-meaning friends and family.

'Seriously? You're going back to them again? What else do they have to do to prove they are a complete waste of space?' or 'Here you go again! If there is someone you can find who will treat you badly and reduce your self-esteem to the size of a molecule, you will find them,' or the more nurturing, 'Let me help you find someone decent for a change. I've got a lovely friend who would be perfect for you.'

These comments all sound helpful and may even be right, but whenever I have expressed similar well-meant views in the past to friends (never to clients), the responses have ranged from the rebellious child telling me to shove them where the sun doesn't shine to the compliant and appeasing child crumpling in a heap and crying, agreeing with everything I've just said. In either case, they ignored my advice and carried on doing exactly the same thing, whether in their current relationship or the next one.

It is so frustrating when people simply refuse to accept your well-intentioned advice. If they accepted it, then everything would be OK in the world, wouldn't it? Hmm, imposed values and limiting beliefs with a side order of my rules for table five, please.

The trouble is, well-meaning comments from people who see our patterns repeating themselves all carry a lot of judgement too, not only about the person we are with, but also about us for putting up with them. We can feel deeply hurt, embarrassed and even shamed by the criticism, but unless we get to the root of why we make those choices, we are likely to keep repeating them. This ultimately risks us rejecting the ones who love us because it becomes too difficult to be around them and their disapproval.

So, what are some of the common triggers and behaviour patterns our friends and family witness?

In my case, my loved ones repeatedly saw me with men who were simply not available. Usually this unavailability was on an emotional level, but occasionally it was on a practical one too. Friends saw me constantly making excuses for how dismissive, unreliable and downright insulting my partners' behaviour was. Instead of having the self-confidence to walk away, I tried to adjust my own behaviour, spending hours analysing then excusing the 'why' of their behaviour as though understanding it would make it OK. After all, all they needed was acceptance, wasn't it?

I have worked with many clients who have struggled to walk away from someone who is behaving badly. Quite often, they are seemingly confident, popular and intelligent people who make well-informed decisions in every aspect of their life apart from romance. When we're uncovering the patterns behind this, we find key beliefs such as, 'It is wrong to give up on someone' or 'What kind of person would I be if I walked away when he/she needs me?' or 'Love will conquer all' holding them back. These beliefs may all seem logical, but the programme that is really running is usually, 'I cannot cope with not being seen as perfect by always doing or saying the right thing in the right way at the right time,' or 'I am too scared of rejection to put boundaries around how this person treats me,' or 'If I don't believe in them, no one else will, and isn't that what love is all about?'

The last one is often a deeply ingrained belief and will trigger certain reactions. Continually loving someone while getting little back can pay off if that person realises they need to own their issues and do something about them. But more often than not, it rarely works out and we become even more damaged by the process. For friends and family, this is hard to watch, which is not helped by the fact that they may have seen it countless times before.

The impact of a partner's damaging behaviours can lead you to wonder:

♡ Am I sexy enough?

♡ Am I being loving/supportive/understanding/funny enough?

♡ Am I sassy or confident enough?

All these can trigger the compliant and appeasing child seeking out strong and domineering partners so they can feel loved and needed. Or they might go the other way, triggering more rebellious responses such as, 'I am going to celebrate being with an unavailable man because that is safe and keeps things in my control.

SUMMARY & QUESTIONS

What makes a relationship 'wrong'? In whose opinion is it wrong?

By looking at the patterns and triggers within the relationships and the type of partners I chose, I examined what feelings consistently came up for me and how these were meeting my needs in both healthy and unhealthy ways. Sometimes, the thrill of excitement felt great, but more often than not I had feelings of anxiety, worry, stress and fear that I didn't fit in with what I thought my partner wanted.

Peer pressure also plays a big part here. The opinion of our friends and family may sometimes override our own instincts and judgment, particularly if they have very strong values and opinions about right and wrong types that may trigger our set responses. It is also quite often the case that others see no problem with expressing their opinion as to your choice of partner but will not necessarily welcome you expressing yours about theirs. Churchill summed this up by saying;

*'Everyone is in favour of free speech.
But some people's idea of it is that they are free to
say what they like, but if anyone else says
anything back, that is an outrage.'*

Quite often, we get our need for variety and uncertainty met by choosing relationships that put us on an emotional rollercoaster. If certainty is our driver, we may choose people who either offer us little emotional range or give us so much uncertainty that our need for certainty leads us to become controlling of both our own and others' emotions and reactions. Either way, our sense of significance very much hangs on how the other person views and treats us rather than how we view or treat ourselves.

You. What are your particular patterns and triggers? What type of person are you attracted to? What do they give you in terms of meeting your needs?

Do you thrive on uncertainty and variety so deliberately choose partners who are only going to be short term or who don't require much emotional commitment? Do you treat every relationship and encounter as more emotionally charged than it is and quickly become obsessive when your partner doesn't return the same depth of commitment? Do you spend hours agonising over every little thing that you and they have said or done?

Do you deliberately stick to people you know your family and friends will approve of, even though you find them dull? Do you believe that all relationships are about settling? Do you consistently put your own needs aside to rescue others and therefore are only attracted to 'victim' types?

Are you always blaming others for your choices, saying, 'I don't know why this keeps happening to me'? Do you constantly seem to meet the wrong type? Well, they seem to keep meeting you too, so there's the reason you find each other.

Others. It leads to positive growth in relationships if you have a good understanding of what drives your partner and how they want/expect their needs to be met. The question is, as with your own needs, are these expectations reasonable and realistic?

You may be triggered by old patterns of responses that lead you to want to fix and change or become compliant to the will of others. You may also be influenced by the values and beliefs of others who push you into either beginning a relationship, or ending one that doesn't fit with their idea of what is right for you.

Whatever the trigger, the rule of thumb is that in the adult state, you take responsibility for how you feel and act, and allow others to do the same. Only you can decide if the patterns you are recognising mean you wish to stay and work through them or choose to walk away.

Understanding. What are your patterns? What type of partner do you keep looking for? Is this a pattern you could change if it no longer serves you and what you want in your life now?

Who do you know who already role models this? What could you learn from how they treat other people and, more importantly, themselves?

What could you do to learn more about your own needs and patterns in order to become open to trying different types of relationships? They may make you feel better.

The more you look after your own well-being, the more likely you are to choose relationships that will enhance how you feel rather than detract from it.

Relationships can be a bit like types of food. If you regard the people you meet as being part of a giant smorgasbord, you can open up your choices based on what you have already tried. You may choose to stick to healthy foods which will make you feel good, but may be a little dull. Or you may choose from the naughty foods platter. These foods are great to enjoy as a treat now and then, but not so great as a consistent diet. Or you could take a risk and try something completely new. That food may then be added to your healthy or naughty table, or become part of your 'banned' list if the experience is so toxic you never want to eat it again.

Choices, choices.

THREE

Understanding The Imposter Syndrome

Would the real you please stand up?

'I'm sorry, but it has come to our attention that you are here under false pretences. You are not who you claim to be and therefore we must ask you to leave.'

Oh, bugger! What, again? I thought that in this relationship I could finally pull off being smart, sexy, together and confident – the only woman on the entire planet my partner would want. Roll end credits as, yet again, this hope is dashed.

Welcome to the world of the Imposter Syndrome.

Most people have experienced the Imposter Syndrome. It's when you have that awful, gut-wrenching feeling inside that you do not deserve to be doing what you are doing. You shouldn't be what you are being because you don't believe you have the necessary credentials. You're feeling totally out of your league, constantly waiting for someone to find you out and expose you for the fraud you really are.

The term 'Imposter Syndrome' was first introduced in 1978 by clinical psychologists Dr Pauline R. Clance and Suzanne A Imes based on their research into how some successful people dismissed their accomplishments, despite external evidence showing that they were perfectly competent. In relationship terms, this can lead us to never recognising our true qualities and successes because we focus only on what we feel we are failing at.

This shows up with lots of my clients. I can especially relate to comments such as, 'If I tried to be sexier, do you think he would love me more?'; 'She thinks I'm this strong, dynamic executive, but I feel really unsure of myself with her at times'; 'He doesn't like it when I get emotional so I never really show my feelings with him'. And then we get back to the good old Transactional Analysis triggers: 'He only responds to me and listens when I cry and he feels he has to take care of me' (needy child); 'He won't do anything unless I nag him. I just want to be relaxed and playful with him like I used to be' (Critical parent); 'She says she wants me to be there for her, but when I try to be attentive, she gets irritated and withdrawn' (rebellious child).

The Halo Complex – when we enviously admire someone we feel has their whole life sorted – feeds into this. If we constantly compare ourselves unfavourably with others, coveting the qualities and attributes we feel they have in their relationships, we believe that we can never be as good as them. We see them as being 'perfect' and beat ourselves up for not being the same.

Neither the Imposter Syndrome nor the Halo Complex is conducive to developing the attitude of it being OK not to be perfect. They can in fact generate some pretty damaging behaviours within our relationships because we are operating on very little self-esteem and placing unrealistic expectations on how our needs are met.

In my own case, I decided at a young age that I didn't feel comfortable being flirty or sexy because it didn't feel safe for me. I then set about cultivating my 'best friend' persona, studiously avoided trying to attract anyone I considered out of my league. If, for some strange reason, I did catch the attention of one of these wonderful creatures, I would unconsciously sabotage any chance of a relationship by becoming needy, clingy and jealous if they paid attention to anyone else.

Meanwhile, the Halo Complex was kicking in nicely. I tortured myself with the fact that I wasn't anywhere near as pretty, thin, sexy, fun and desirable as my friends, or the countless celebrities I compared myself to. Who would possibly want to be with me while that lot were around?

I would demonstrate this by saying things like, 'Do you think she is pretty? She's really sexy, isn't she?' meaning, 'I've seen you looking and I can't bear that I'm nowhere near as pretty and sexy as she is, so please tell me that you prefer me. Even if I won't believe you.' Or, 'So, what is it you like about being with me?' meaning, 'Please tell me that you want to be with me because I am the woman of your dreams, even though I am only showing the sides of myself I feel confident with while expecting you to guess what reassurance I truly need. Oh, and I may well give you lots of mixed messages in response so you are never sure of where you stand with me either. Or, 'What do your friends think of me? Do they prefer me to your ex?' meaning, 'If your friends and family like me then you are bound to want to stay with me, even though I'm terrified that your ex is much more your type than I am.' And of course I can't trust you to make your own adult decision about that.

I was completely missing the point that the Halo Complex makes us blind to the fact that everyone is human. Just because someone seems to have it all in the looks, sex appeal and romance department, it doesn't mean they aren't feeling like an imposter too.

I remember feeling a mix of shock and relief when I read that Cheryl Cole's husband had cheated on her. Wow, if someone that gorgeous can't keep her man, what hope do the rest of us have? Then there followed gleeful joy at seeing her halo slip, compounded by the media with comments such as, 'Well, she may be pretty, but he strayed for a reason. She must be a nightmare to live with.'

I must say here that I really like Cheryl. She is totally upfront about the fact that she is gorgeous, but that she is also human with hang-ups like everyone else. She is honest about her mistakes and wants to be loved and accepted for who she is, warts and all. A good role model, I would say.

We delete, distort and generalise what we experience as a way of maintaining our fixed belief about who we think we are, or should be. For example, in my quest to be seen as the funny friend rather than the sexy minx, I put on a show. I would cheerfully ignore any experiences of men who, despite my best efforts, did find me sexy and flirty and wanted to explore that with me. Comments such as, 'You are really lovely, you know,' or 'You are so sexy' would be met with, 'Oh, bless you! So, how is your mum?' Or, my then behaving like a mum figure.

I would also distort what I was experiencing by misreading signals given by others. If a man made a flirty comment to me, I would assume that he was just being kind and set about re-establishing the girl-next-door persona, removing all possible minxiness from my demeanour. Alternatively, if I really liked him, I would go to the other extreme and misinterpret everything he said as a come-on, only to realise my mistake and curl up with shame and embarrassment. That would teach me for thinking I was something I'm not!

People generalise, making blanket statements such as, 'Men only like certain types of women,' or 'Why do women only like men who treat them badly?' or 'Passion never lasts in relationships, everyone knows that,'

In response to friends who told me, each time I was lamenting another romantic disaster, I would say, 'But I'm scared he won't love me if he knows the real me!' or 'But I don't want him to think I'm being childish or stroppy if I say or do...' or 'I'd love to be myself, but who the hell am I?'

Who indeed?

I love one of the coaching strategies advocated by Tony Robbins. Find an example of someone you admire and find out about their habits so you can emulate what they do. Now, this may sound like stalking behaviour. It may even sound like just another way of being an imposter, but not necessarily. The trick is to recognise how you feel while you are emulating them. What barriers or negative feelings come up? What is behind those barriers?

Other coaches, such as Fiona Harrold, advocate taking on the role of someone with the traits you admire as a stepping stone for building a bridge between where you are now and where you want to be. The more you practise, the more natural it will become, and the more you can acknowledge the positive experiences and feedback rather than feeling inauthentic.

My friends love it when I put on my 'minxy' persona. Then I am flirty and exude confidence. I give the impression that I don't care what others think because I am entirely at ease in my own skin and do not need to compare myself to them. I must admit, sometimes I am just acting, but at other times this is how I genuinely feel. Either way, others respond to me in the same way. I get to build up my bank account of validating experiences that lead to me feeling more significant. The genuine confidence I gain as a result is what matters.

Learn to trust yourself. Develop the intention to explore the different sides of yourself.

For example, I coached a young man recently who is talented, funny, confident and intelligent. However, he lacked confidence in approaching women and feared he was always seen as the 'good friend'. Alternatively, he only attracted girls who didn't stimulate him intellectually.

We talked about what he needed to do to feel valued and certain of himself. I asked what kinds of men he admired and why. He replied that he admired the men he saw in the City who exuded confidence and power, not just by the way they dressed and held themselves, but because they always looked so at ease in their own company. This was something he felt too scared to do because he felt he would be perceived as a loner rather than confident or powerful.

I suggested that over the course of a week, he got comfortable with sitting alone for short periods of time in public places. He could use the time to read his paper, check through work or simply relax and observe. With practice, he realised that far from feeling like the loner/loser, he came to enjoy and value the solitude and the opportunity it gave him to think. The loner perception had only ever been in his head, and by changing his actions, he changed his perceptions.

I was delighted to learn that not only had fellow businessmen begun to strike up conversations with him, but a few weeks later, a girl approached him, saying that she had noticed him in the bar a few times and wondered if he worked locally. He confidently replied that he did, and there followed a great conversation that led to them going on a date.

SUMMARY & QUESTIONS

Most of us at some point feel like we are imposters, especially within relationships, and this always comes down to our need for significance. The rules we create for feeling valued, accepted or admired all stem from how we compare ourselves either to others or to a perfect 'ideal'.

We may feel we cannot deviate from set 'roles' or 'personas' we create as they give us control over how others view and treat us, even if they aren't how we actually want to be. But personas are safe, far less risky than exposing ourselves in different ways and being rejected or ridiculed as a result.

Exploring and celebrating the different parts of yourself doesn't make you an imposter. It's all part of finding out who you are and being comfortable with those different aspects of yourself. Then you can create ways to feel comfortable being yourself in a loving and trusting relationship, the first one being with yourself.

You. It is important to get clear on how and why you are judging yourself. Are you seeing yourself as others see you? Are the values behind your preferred persona your own or being imposed by others? Are you constantly trying to present yourself in a certain way, staying safe but not necessarily happy?

The danger here is that you're potentially missing out on having experiences that will help you develop more certainty and confidence from within yourself.

How are you regularly behaving to get attention? Is your pattern to be needy or quiet and submissive? Are you judgmental of others, gaining significance by tearing them down for presenting themselves in a particular way when, in reality, you wish you could behave in the same way? Emulating the traits and qualities of those you admire and having the Halo Complex are two different things.

Why do you admire certain people? What would being more like them give you? What needs would you be meeting, and how positively or negatively would this impact on how you feel about yourself?

What could you do differently to feel better about yourself and not be so judgmental when comparing yourself to others?

Others. The NLP phrase, 'Spot it and you've got it' really comes into play here. We are often highly critical of others who demonstrate traits we dislike, going into judgmental parent mode and chastising them for being too attention seeking or false.

This is how our behaviours get triggered by others. What mode do we enter when faced with behaviours from others that we don't like or understand? Very common is the stroppy foot-stamping response. We demand that they get with the programme and feel, think and act in the way we consider best. This invariably leads to confrontation, misunderstanding and further cracks in how we judge ourselves and others.

How much of this is because we fear that we too possess the flaws we are criticising? Might others be judging us almost as harshly as we judge ourselves? How secretly envious are we? Do we wish we too could unleash our inner vixen or macho man, exuding the charisma that would have everyone falling at our feet?

Don't assume that others see you the way you see yourself, or that those who exude magnetism don't feel they compare unfavourably to others. We all have our flaws and our issues, and most of us judge without knowing the full story.

You don't know how comfortable you may be with exploring the different sides of yourself until you try. Then it is possible to look at patterns. Whom do you compare yourself to? What is it that makes you feel you are an imposter? Simply accept that you are human with different parts to your personality, just like anyone else.

Do an audit of all the successes you have had in your relationships. When did you feel good about expressing different sides of yourself to others? What were you feeling? What side of you were you expressing? How did this impact on others? What effect did this have on your self-confidence?

How often could you try on a role that felt good? Not so that you stay stuck in acting out the role, but so you can feel confident in trying it for size. What new experiences could you attract?

Understanding. Nothing is fixed. Different people bring out different sides of us, hence the need for variety and connection.

When we connect with someone, it may be because they appeal to a side of us we want to explore. If we express that side, it doesn't mean that we are being imposters. However, it also doesn't mean that we will constantly want to display that side. It's all about balance.

Think of your different friends and the different needs they help you meet. Who do you go to for uncomplicated fun or gossip? For more deep and meaningful conversations? Who do you share common interests with? Who do you try new things with? Who do you tell your secrets to? Who are you the sensible comforter for? Who describes you as the zany one? The truth is we are different people in different relationships, and accepting this is key. It is how we feel, and the response we get from others, that counts.

Perhaps if I had learnt more from my earlier relationships, I would have been more open to demonstrating the different sides of myself, including the minx. Instead, I hid behind being the caring, sensible fixer friend. It may also have saved me from the embarrassment of a fit of frustration when yet another guy in the pub told me I was sweet while describing my friend as hot and asking, 'Is she single?'

In response, I drunkenly stood on a table and yelled, 'I am not a teddy bear, I am a woman!'

Enough said.

FOUR

The Ex-Files And How To Deal With Them

'I do hope you have been kind enough to give her a cardigan. Why? Well, it must get incredibly chilly up on that pedestal you have put her on!'

Not one of my finest moments. This outburst was the culmination of yet another conversation about boyfriend's ex. In hindsight, there could be no positive response to that comment as it was designed to convey exactly how much resentment I felt towards her.

And what had this fair maid done to deserve such caustic sarcasm? Why, she had the temerity to have not only come before me, but also be a lovely person whom he still felt affection for. The fact that he was also still in regular contact with her did not make for a pleasant scene. This scene was to repeat on an increasingly regular basis and was ultimately responsible for the demise of our relationship.

So what is it about ex partners that gets us so rattled? Is the need to feel more valued, more loved, than the one before down to our own insecurities, or is it the behaviours of our partner? Or is it a combination of the two?

In my example, the main issue was that I had discovered lengthy emails that made it abundantly clear my partner was struggling to tell his ex the truth about me and our relationship. When I questioned him about this, he said it was because she had not wanted to break up and he was trying to spare her feelings. This in itself was not anything to condemn him for, but it still had me jumping up and down in outrage, screeching, 'Oh really? Sparing her feelings, are we. And what about mine? You are with me! Tell her the truth. If she has any self-respect, she will go and find herself a new man and leave us alone.'

Well, how could he resist me at this moment? Especially when I followed this comment with, 'And what does that say about you, eh? Are you so much of a wimp that you can't just tell her to get lost?'

Oh, I'm sorry, are those your genitals now rolling across the floor because I have thoroughly emasculated you? Have I totally undermined your ability to think and act for yourself? I do apologise. Let me now switch to compliant child so you can recognise me as the vulnerable one who needs looking after. And we can forget all about it, until the next time. Which of course will happen on a regular basis until we get adult and resolve this properly.

In my defence, my insecurity largely came from the fact that he had become distant and withdrawn from me, which was confusing as we had recently moved in together. Nothing was happening as I felt it should and my outbursts were the result of increasing uncertainty about him and us.

It has taken a lot of soul searching to come to terms with why I felt so threatened by her and reacted so badly. Yes, he was at fault too. His behaviours contributed to the insecurity and confusion I felt, but it wasn't his intention to hurt me. He was simply doing his best to manage us both and compartmentalise, as lovely fellas are apt to do.

What is really tragic is that this set the tone for the rest of our relationship as we never really regained the trust we'd had. In my continued sense of outrage, I believed he now owed it to me to make up for his mistake, and I continued to punish him by never letting him forget it. I created a lot of uncertainty for him as I swung between being highly critical and highly nurturing, when what I really wanted was to create more certainty and connection for us both.

It was my friend and fellow coach, Liz, who pulled me up on this one day. I was at her house and had just finished a call with the soon-to-be-ex, who was away for the weekend. It had not been a pleasant conversation:

'So, who are you with exactly?'

'The usual crowd, I told you that.'

'Have you written that letter to *her* yet?'

'No, I'm away, and besides, I need to have time to think about what to say.'

'Oh, really? I thought I had made it clear what you had to say. Why is it you are still more worried about hurting her feelings than mine?'

And so on and so on. By the end of the call, I had done a fairly good job of making him feel miserable and guilty, and I felt totally justified in my rant.

Liz then looked at me and quietly said, 'Bec, just how many hoops are you wanting him to jump through to make up for his mistake?'

'But he has hurt me!' I spluttered in indignation.

'Yes. But he has owned why and is doing his best to put it right. Why are you not giving him the time and space to do that in his own way? You are punishing him for not doing it your way and pushing him to the point where I fear your relationship won't be able to survive.'

She was absolutely right, but it still took me a long time to stop the destructive behaviours as I was convinced they were justified. Despite both of our best efforts, the relationship couldn't survive my constant need to control and punish and his increasing frustration at not feeling he ever did enough to make me happy.

I have now discovered through my work with clients just how common these behaviours are among couples. Comments and questions from both male and female clients have included:

'I know it is wrong, but I have been checking her texts and WhatsApp messages because I don't believe she is telling the truth.'

'He is evasive whenever I bring his ex up. If they are really just friends, then why can't I meet her?'

'She says she doesn't have feelings for him like that anymore, so why is it she still wants to spend so much time with him?'

'She's still invited to his family events and she has asked him to be her plus one at a wedding for mutual friends. Am I wrong to say I don't feel comfortable with that?'

'Her mother still talks about him and how much she liked him.'

'Whenever I try to talk to him about his ex, he gets all defensive and says I am being paranoid. Why can't I trust that although he still cares about her, they are only friends now?'

All of the above represent the breaking of the one golden rule in relationships: love the one you're with, putting them first. If this isn't happening, then both of you need to take ownership of the behaviours or feelings that are blocking it.

This is where understanding the key differences between men and women really comes in handy. Tony Robbins is masterful at explaining quite complex psychology in simple and relatable terms.

> *'What has to happen for you and your partner's need for Certainty, Variety, Significance, Love and Connection, Growth and Contribution to be met?*
>
> **TONY ROBBINS**

The assumption here is that these will be met in healthy and realistic ways that will enhance both your and your partner's well-being, yet in my own experience and in my work with clients, this is not always the case.

So what about when we become the ex?

I have long been a fan of *Sex And The City* and the character of Carrie Bradshaw. In one episode, she confronts some male friends of her recent ex when she cannot believe they are not horrified at the way he broke up with her, which was by Post-it note, saying, 'I'm sorry, I can't. Don't hate me'.

When one of the men mumbles something along the lines of, 'Well, you know, break-ups are hard and sometimes we just don't know what to say. Plus, you women tend to get all mad and crazy irrational', how she responds is a masterclass in being adult. In a nutshell, she explains that this 'crazy behaviour' wouldn't happen if men could simply be honest about wanting to break up and treat their ex with the respect she deserves. Finding cowardly ways to avoid dealing with the ex, face to face, is what makes her behave in crazy ways.

Well, all I can say is she was a lot politer than I would have been.

This is an excellent point very well presented. And one that could be taken on by both men and women.

In my case, what was I doing to meet my need for certainty? Well, trying to control everything, for one thing. I needed to feel certain that I mattered to my boyfriend more than anyone else and that he would communicate that to everyone, especially his ex. But rather than explain how I felt, I chose instead to become extremely critical and judgmental about her, which spoke volumes to him. Clearly I respected neither his original choice to be with her nor his ability to make me feel loved in the way I expected.

To regain his own sense of certainty, he hid things from me and tried to please both of us in order to feel he was doing the right thing. Well, that clearly didn't work.

What about variety? The roller coaster of emotions, mostly negative ones, created lots of uncertainty. He could never be sure how I was going to react as I swung between being adult and understanding one minute to screeching harpy the next. Far from the polarity and spark that Robbins advocates for healthy relationships – creating variety and surprise for each other in fun ways to sustain passion and interest – the level of uncertainty created by both of us meant that passion and interest melted as fast as the buckets of Haagen-Dazs I was consuming on a regular basis.

Love and Connection. I needed to feel heard and understood, and so did he. Instead, I felt sidelined and he felt disrespected, so the love and connection became a battleground. Who could prove themselves more in terms of what they felt they were 'owed' by the other?

Significance. Both men and women want to feel that they are able to make their partner happy while also feeling their partner wants the same. How this actually plays out differs from couple to couple. Tony Robbins explains this key difference as that men may need to gain significance from their partner by feeling valued in their role as strong supporter while also feeling trusted in how they do this.

Some women may feel the need for more reassurance or communication to feel valued at certain times. This may play out by appearing needy and demanding whereas the communication between them may have become difficult. In my case, I simply wanted to feel that I was more important than the ex but didn't know how to ask for that in clear and reasonable ways. My ex felt I was being insensitive and unreasonable by asking him to prove himself to me in ways that made him feel uncomfortable. The result was neither of us feeling the strength and support from the other we each craved.

SUMMARY & QUESTIONS

When we have loved and lost, it can be tricky to recalibrate our feelings. Sometimes the pain or rejection felt after a break up can leave us with lingering emotional triggers that make us lose perspective about how we want and expect our needs to be met. Recognising this can allow us to reflect on what was and wasn't within our control and the lessons we may need to learn about the expectations we place on ourselves and others.

How reasonable or realistic are we being in how we want our needs to be met? What damage are we potentially doing to our sense of love and connection? How do our expectations help the relationship to grow? How are we maintaining the healthy sense of variety to keep things sparky?

Many people want their partners to feel a little bit jealous because, in their eyes, this proves that they really matter. They find it flattering and endearing. Too much jealousy, however, turns people from being endearingly romantic to downright psychotic and controlling. Not so pleasant for either partner.

You. Unless this is the first relationship for you and your partner, then you will have had previous partners.

How open are you to the fact that your partner may well have loved others before you and what emotions does that trigger in you? Are you ok with the fact that they have loved and lost before and that this bears no relation on how they feel about you as their current partner? Or does this trigger intense feelings of insecurity and lead to behaviours that demonstrate your lack of trust or self-confidence that then require lots of reassurance in ways that may not always be reasonable or realistic?

Even when the break up is mutual, though especially when it isn't, how do you cope when your partner moves on to someone else? I really struggled with this as it brought up the triggers of rejection and not being good enough. My head may have been ok with the fact that it was right we both moved on, but my emotions and heart said something completely different. It took me several months to work through the painful emotions of feeling that to move on so quickly he could never really have loved me in the first place, and that the new partner clearly deserved his love more than me. In my desire to appear externally adult and perfect I refused to acknowledge these feelings and chose instead to express my hurt and pain by being angry or dismissive of him and the time we spent together.

What has been your pattern in relationships and how they have ended? How willing are you to look at how your own feelings and emotional triggers may have created similar patterns and outcomes that have left you feeling mistrustful or lacking in self-worth? What expectations do you place on your partner to convince you that they love you? Does this perhaps lead to jealous or possessive behaviours and create a situation where, as in my case, your partner actually can't win because you are denying them the right to deal with their own emotions and past relationships in an adult way?

Have you perhaps made a key decision in your past about how relationships are or should be and then look for evidence to support that, no matter what the truth may be? What might it be like if we allowed ourselves to consider different possibilities and to accept that to do so we may need to do a little work or make some different choices?

Others. People make mistakes. For all sorts of reasons, they mess up, but how we respond to those mistakes determines the relationship and how we feel about ourselves and others. By continually forcing others to jump through hoops to make us happy, we will only create misery on both sides. Being forgiving and trusting that the ex is an ex for a reason, then openly discussing our partners' behaviours in relation to the ex in an adult way is key.

How reasonable are their behaviours towards their ex? Is the communication they have with them open and honest and clear that you, as current partner are the priority?

How do they talk about their ex? Is it with affection for the time shared and care for the person they still have feelings for though not the same feelings as for you?

Are they secretive about their ex? Do you feel side-lined by your partner and/or their family in how they still interact with them or refer to them? What expectations are they placing on you in understanding that they are still friends? What behaviour do each of them display? Is it respectful to you and your relationship? What does that actually need to look like for you to feel comfortable?

With all relationships involving the words 'I love you', it is important to honour what you had if the relationship breaks down, however short term it may have been.

Recognise other people's right to choose. If they are choosing to be with you, then trust that and don't allow your own insecurities to tip you over the edge into being needy and controlling. Otherwise this will quickly erode the spark that got you together in the first place.

If, though, your partner's communication and actions regarding their ex are clearly undermining your relationship, then you need to own that, for whatever reason, they are not committed to you. For your own sense of worth and well-being, I would recommend you choose to walk away and be with someone who genuinely wants to be with you.

Having said that, the same questions have to be applied to others as to the ones to yourself above? What are their emotional triggers and responses? What has been the pattern of their previous break ups and what type of key decisions have they made as to what they feel an ideal relationship should look like?

How is your behaviour affecting your partner? Are you making it impossible for them to feel they are doing anything positive for you? Are you showing how much you value them? By asking them to completely deny ever having had an ex let alone any continuing feelings of care, does this trigger behaviours in both of you that erodes the trust?

Understanding. No one is perfect, so we need to be more forgiving and cut a little slack. Also, not all relationships are perhaps destined to be 'the one' or even long term. In any relationship, it is the hope that each partner will be treated with respect and trust with open and adult communication. It is also about awareness and intent. If the intent behind your partner's behaviour is misguided rather than deliberately deceptive or dismissive, then allow for the fact that we all make mistakes. It is more important to look at the relationship as a whole.

In general, are both of you making a genuine effort to make the other feel prioritised? Is the trust level high enough for you to give your partner space to deal with difficult emotions concerning their ex, providing this does not constantly impact negatively on you?

Each relationship is unique. What is enough reassurance and trust for one couple is not necessarily enough for another. The important thing is to get clear on the genuine intent behind the words and actions. If your partner's words consistently don't match their actions, then it is time to look at both of your behaviours. How adult are each of you being? How realistic is it to give your partner what they need to feel valued and safe? How are you feeling most of the time?

This is all part of what rules we individually make and use in our relationships and how open we are to being more flexible about them. Accepting that the word 'love' means different things to each of us in terms of how it is expressed can save a lot of mental anguish. This applies while we are in the relationship and if we are an ex. What feels right and normal for how you would behave and treat others may not be seen in the same way by them. The point is to recognise our own patterns and triggers and also those in the partners we attract; and learn from them so we can make different choices and save ourselves unnecessary anguish.

FIVE

Spotting The Toxic Relationship

'But if I don't believe in them, how will they ever believe in themselves and know that they deserve to be loved?'

Feeling sick to my stomach at what I was about to do, I banged on the door of where I knew my partner was having dinner with friends on the pretext that he had offered to help me move some furniture and I needed it done that night. As he hadn't been in contact, I had to come and find him to know whether or not to ask someone else.

Welcome to the world of the toxic relationship. Now what I have just said doesn't, in itself, particularly raise any alarm bells. At that moment, there could be any number of reasons why he hadn't been in contact and why I felt the need to seek him out. I should now add that he was having dinner with mutual friends, and he had said my reason for not being there was that I was busy. I wasn't. I didn't even know about it, and I hadn't heard from him for two days, despite his last text being a cheery, 'Love you and see you soon'.

As a grown woman, I now want to shout, 'For the love of God, what was wrong with you?' The first clue that I wasn't making a good move came from how wretched I was feeling physically. And unless he had mysteriously lost the use of his fingers, surely he would have been in contact if he had wanted to? Well of course he would, only he never did unless it suited him.

So what happened? He tersely got rid of me from the now very embarrassed dinner party with the promise that he would come round in an hour. I spent the next hour absolutely dreading seeing him. Why was I feeling like a desperately needy child, willing to go to any lengths to get some attention from him? Was I so hooked on the drama and uncertainty he created? Why was I ignoring how often I felt completely wretched with him, and how exhausted I was by constantly having to adapt around his moods? And on the times I did explode, he would choose to walk away from me, saying he couldn't put up with my unreasonable behaviour and demands. Would the rare times he did make me feel special and loved happen more often if I never expressed my hurt and anger?

I had been in a relationship with him on and off for nearly three years. We met at a dance and he literally swept me off my feet that first evening, telling me I was fantastic and that being with me made him feel like a teenager again. I'd also had a crush on him for a number of years. But by the second date, the pattern for what was to come was already emerging. He was late, calling after I'd been waiting an hour to say he had been held up with his son. Could we postpone? To make it up to me, he'd take me to a gallery opening the following night.

Now my alarm bells were already ringing and at that point I wasn't really fussed if I saw him again. But my ever-present need to seek validation that the loveliness of the first date hadn't just been my imagination reared up again, and off I went on a three year journey that had me doubting my sanity by the end of it.

It is very difficult to be light-hearted about being in a toxic relationship as the impact and consequences can be so extreme. More often than not, toxic relationships come about because we choose to judge others by the same standards as we would judge ourselves.

For example, I worked with a young male client who constantly questioned himself and his partner, saying, 'She said she understands how I feel when she behaves like that, but she goes and does it again. Then she blames me for being paranoid and unfair. How can someone say they love you and want to be with you, then do that?'

And this truly is difficult to understand when we are expecting the other person to feel and express love in the same way as we do. Especially when our ways come under what we consider to be 'normal' within a relationship.

Eventually, this client developed the strength to accept that, for him, love simply wasn't enough. To keep loving that person, he increasingly had to not love himself. After a lot of soul searching as to why he stayed and which needs he was meeting by doing so, he chose to walk away.

It took a lot of willingness on his part to recognise how his behaviours had been enabling those of his partner. By taking on so much ownership and responsibility to make the relationship work, he actually took away any opportunity for her to do so, and they stayed stuck in an increasingly toxic loop that left them both miserable.

When I work with clients, their stories always bring up similar experiences from my own past, which is why I understood only too well the reasons behind what each of them was doing in that particular case. Looking at the patterns of my relationships, I had to recognise that I was attracted to, and was also attracting, people with narcissistic qualities.

It can be easy to lump together a set of behaviours that define a narcissist, summed up as, 'I love me, who do you love?' to explain their perceived ultra-selfishness. But the opposite is true. Narcissists tend to do anything but love themselves. Instead, they are stuck in a pattern of being forever in 'fight' mode as their response to early trauma, displaying behaviours that appear cold, uncaring and defensive. Mix that with someone whose typical response is to walk on eggshells and over-please, and a mutually unfulfilling relationship is born.

Everyone has experienced trauma of some kind, and our patterns of thinking, feeling and behaving come from how we have either dealt or not dealt with the effects of that. Feeling unlovable, unworthy and assuming you will always be rejected are all typical reactions. For our own well-being, as well as that of others, it is important to recognise that the root of our behaviours is the need to feel loved and understood, even though the resultant behaviours often make it difficult for that need to be fulfilled.

So how does this show up in our relationships? How can we spot if the relationship we are in has become or is heading towards being toxic? What can we do about it?

Well, in my case, I chose to completely ignore how often he lied to me or pretended to others that I didn't exist, and how he would punish me emotionally by sulking and withdrawing if I dared to challenge him on this. I quickly learnt that to be certain of having him around, I had to be cheery and fun, and if I challenged him at all, it would have to be done in a way that he found endearing and childlike. Any attempt at being adult and asking him to take responsibility for his own actions was met with either complete stonewalling or reasoned arguments as to why I was in the wrong.

I must own that I didn't help myself here as I too was inconsistent in the messages I gave him. I would complain that he didn't treat me well, but I chose to stay with him. I would grumble to others and seek their advice, then promptly ignore it if he showed a glimmer of treating me well for a change. I would say what I wanted from him, and then not give him the opportunity to follow through. Because I was so convinced that he couldn't be trusted and would fail, I simply wouldn't give him the space and time to try.

It probably didn't help that I also slammed him by saying, 'Oh, really? You're trying, are you? Well, do you wake up in the morning and try to take a pee? No, you just do it! But you can't, can you?'

I will always remember one particular night. I was staying over, and we'd had another difficult evening. Rather than telling him outright how I was feeling, I had been making little digs which then caused him to lose his rag and be cold and distant. As usual, I said I wouldn't put up with being treated like that anymore, but then found an excuse to stay.

His comment on this occasion was, 'You know, I would have far more respect for you if you had the courage of your convictions and actually followed through on what you said.'

It was not long after this that the fateful gatecrashing of the dinner party occurred. Finally, the pattern had got too much and I recognised that I was allowing this toxic relationship to take over my life.

What makes it hard to get to this point is that the people we are with are never all bad. We become deeply moved by our compassion for whatever trauma or experience they have been through, and that makes us want to hang in there and believe that, with enough love and patience, all will turn out OK. Sometimes it does, but we have to weigh that chance against the cost to ourselves, and to them, of the process of getting there.

For me, the moment to call it quits came that night. As he was leaving with yet another snide comment about how embarrassing I was and how I needed to get a grip, I did just that. I got a very strong grip on his collar and put my foot on his backside, firmly propelling him out of the door. He landed in a sprawled heap on the pavement. End of relationship.

I will for ever remember the huge satisfaction.

SUMMARY & QUESTIONS

You. It would be easy to dismiss this guy as a monster, which of course he wasn't. But the fact that everyone's behaviour is a result of their own level of trauma and their intent is to protect themselves against pain and rejection doesn't mean you have to excuse being treated badly. In fact, that only adds to the problem.

In any relationship it is important to ask how much ownership you habitually take for how others feel and behave. Do you tend to put more emphasis on your desire to fix the other person and be the one who can heal them rather than stepping back and considering how the need to do this may be detrimental to your own well-being and also theirs?

Are you operating from an ingrained value system or belief that we must always put others first and see the good in them even though their behaviour and response consistently contradicts this? Does this cause you to stay in relationships because the importance of not giving up on them overrides the pain and trauma the relationship creates? Having to constantly tread on eggshells to avoid conflict and pain may mean we are most likely to be stuck in appeasing child mode, alternating with critical parent. Occasionally we'll become stroppy, rebellious child, though not too much because of the fear of being rejected.

It is important to recognise and try to meet the needs of your partner as well as have them meet yours, but ask yourself how reasonable those needs are. What is the cost to you and to others around you? By consistently making excuses for and meeting those needs, are you treating them like children who are incapable of taking responsibility for their own actions? Are you being a judgmental parent or a nurturing and appeasing parent?

I had to take ownership of the fact that what was driving me the most was the fear that if I gave up on who I believed he could be, then I might miss out on having the 'ideal' relationship. Even worse, if I chose to walk away, what if he then sought professional help to work through his issues and subsequently found that ideal love with someone else?

Looking after yourself first is not selfish, it is essential.

Others. When we don't distance ourselves from the abusive behaviours of others, we are mirroring their inability to take ownership of feeling happy and treating themselves well. By choosing to stay, we are enabling them to stay the same. Why would they change anything if someone else is willing to take on their responsibility and meet their needs for significance and love? Why would they choose to show you any love and respect when you don't demonstrate that for yourself? What patterns do you see in their behaviours and expectations and is it only with you? Who dies this person and their behaviour remind you of? What responses does this trigger in you and how adult do you feel you are both being?

We may feel that if we step back and show we have more self-respect and self-care than they do, they won't see this as the positive role modelling we intend. Instead, they might regard it as a mirror that further magnifies their own flaws and how terrible they feel about themselves. Their tendency then will be to try and pull us down with them.

However bad our partner's behaviour and however contrite they appear to be, the bottom line is that there is always a pay-off for them staying exactly as they are, even if this makes them and everyone else unhappy. If they behave like a sulky or helpless child, avoiding taking on any adult ownership or responsibility, this appeals to our nurturing parent instinct.

How often do you notice that the more we try and fix, the more they will stay rooted in these behaviours because that keeps their needs being met. The longer we choose to stay, the more damaging their behaviours become, especially when we start to doubt whether we are good enough or loving enough to help them – an illusion they are only too happy for us to have as it keeps them off the hook. We are then likely to behave in ways that seemingly justify their anger or disappointment in us.

If this is the case for you then find support that will help you distance yourself without feeling guilty.

When you are taking care of yourself and exuding genuine confidence and happiness, this impacts on others. You will either attract more of the same, or others will resent it and try to bring you back down. Be strong enough not to let the latter point happen. Accept that walking away does not make you a bad person.

Understanding. When we truly come to terms with recognising our own patterns and needs, the way we allow ourselves to be treated changes. Being loving, hopeful and loyal are all qualities worth keeping, but we need to accept that others may not be in a place where they want to accept or reciprocate those qualities in healthy ways. We don't have to turn into a one person crusade to save them. Nor do we have to ignore behaviours that make us consistently feel unsafe or uncertain. For example, someone who consistently puts you down, verbally or emotionally abuses you or deliberately hides things from you and withdraws from you may well be explained by them being 'just how they are' but these behaviours do not equate to healthy love, trust and respect.

You cannot make someone perfect just because you want them to be. Running a relationship based on the 'ideal' rather than the reality doesn't serve either of you. It is difficult to accept that you may care more for someone than they do for themselves, and that you may be more part of the problem than the solution by choosing to stay.

In this, more than any other relationship dynamic, lies the importance of having the wisdom to know the difference between what you can and cannot change. However different their rules might be for feeling and expressing love and trust, if this is still causing deliberate pain and hurt to someone else and if they are refusing to change, despite the damage they are causing to themselves and others, then that is their choice. You can offer support, guidance and help, but ultimately they must decide for themselves whether they want to take back ownership of their behaviours. You have the choice as to how you want to feel. Is staying in the relationship healthy for you or not?

SIX

Needs Versus Wants

Needs and Wants and the danger of making assumptions

'I'm sorry, but I don't take my Level One Psychic Exam until next week. Until then, please communicate by the usual means.'

I remember working with a client who was indignantly answering my questions about how clear she felt she had been in telling her partner what needed to happen for her to feel more loved and appreciated.

'I have said in no uncertain terms that I want her to pay me more attention, include me more in her life, and show me that she loves me and that I'm important to her.'

'And how did she respond?'

'She said she was trying, but I kept changing the rules.'

When I then asked my client how specific she had been as to what the behaviours she wanted from her partner would look like, she replied, 'Well, it's obvious, isn't it? I shouldn't have to spell it out.'

This began to ring a rather loud bell. From my own experience, I remembered a particularly unhelpful discussion with a past boyfriend. He was complaining that I didn't listen to him and dismissed what he had to say if it didn't match what I wanted to hear.

The conversation culminated in me sarcastically saying, 'Oh, I'm sorry. My copy of the script clearly got delayed in the post. Do come back tomorrow and perhaps we can have a read through then.'

No prizes for guessing which state I was channelling in response to his attempt to be adult.

What my client and I shared was a similar need to create certainty by micromanaging the behaviours and responses of our partners to fit in with our own particular views of the world. While in her case there was equal giving and receiving from both partners of mixed messages which were creating lots of uncertainty in unhealthy ways, I was simply channelling my mum and being hypercritical, judging my boyfriend for simply not knowing what to say and how to behave in the relationship.

Wouldn't it be easier if we were all psychic? Then we wouldn't keep coming a cropper with all the mixed messages and general misunderstandings that plague our relationships. Having said that, I'm not sure if psychic abilities would really help. There would be no filter between what we think and what we actually say (though our faces and bodies can do a lot of the talking for us), and we are often confused ourselves about what we really mean.

I have lost count of the number of times in relationships when I, or my partner, uttered, 'That's not what I said, it's what you heard.'

Hmm. Who is actually in the right? The speaker or the listener?

Well, that depends. How truthful was the speaker in terms of what they really wanted to say? How open was the listener to hearing it?

When we don't read the signs properly because we are too caught up in what we want to see, we lose the ability to recognise that we are all different. Instead of celebrating those differences and finding healthy ways to work with them, we resort to communicating in code that makes perfect sense to us, but not necessarily to the people we are in a relationship with. And who do we then blame for the misunderstanding? Yep, them.

And then there is the magical difference between how men and women communicate, and how we choose to interpret that. There are many books that explore this in more depth, one of the best being John Gray's *Men Are From Mars, Women Are From Venus*. However great that book is, though, what has made it easier for me to interpret my own communication style, and that of people in relationships with me, is connecting it to understanding which of the six needs I am prioritising and the ways in which I expect them to be met.

Not that I mean to make that easy for anyone else to guess, of course, as actually *telling* them would take out all the fun, now, wouldn't it?

I learnt about my inability to communicate my needs the hard way after the relationship I actually credit as being one of my most successful and fulfilling had come to an end. And it was my first ever client I have to thank for this lesson. I was able to have a long chat with my ex and explain my behaviours and how I imagined they had made him feel.

'Ah, that was exactly it!' he exclaimed. 'I felt that no matter what I did, it was never enough for you. All you did was criticise me or become clingy and controlling.'

Ouch! No one ever said that increasing our self-awareness was easy, but it did allow me to look at the intent behind my actions, and this helped me do the same with my client, a lovely man who had come to me because he felt that his life was at a crossroads. He had two teenage children who were becoming more independent, and he had raised them alone since the sad death of his wife a few years earlier. He had since been in an on/off romance with a mutual friend of theirs for the last five years, and it was currently in another off stage.

I asked him if he wanted to resume the relationship with her.

'Yes, I think so, but I fear we want different things.'

'Like what? Can you expand on that?'

'Well, she wants to settle down and be a family unit. I do too, but I find her moods so unpredictable. Mind you, she says the same about me. I just don't know if I'm cut out for being in a relationship as we end up arguing all the time. I then spend more time on my own, and she gets moody and bites my head off or tells me I don't care about her enough when I try to show her I love her.'

'And how do you do that?'

'Well, I give her space and encourage her to do more without me as that's what I'd like her to do for me.'

Oh dear. The classic 'I know how I like to feel loved and valued, so it must be the same for everyone else' syndrome.

I am an affectionate and generous person who loves to feel loved. I like lots of fuss made of me when I feel ill or down and thoughtful gestures to show my partner is thinking of me. When I planned time with my ex, I automatically assumed he liked the same.

Wrong! If he was ill or down he wanted to be left alone. He felt more valued when I gave him space and allowed him the freedom to go out with his own mates sometimes, and he really didn't like the couple thing. He also didn't need gestures such as gifts or extra attention to feel valued, and while affectionate, he didn't like to overdo it.

When I pressed my client to tell me more about the arguments, it transpired they came down, unsurprisingly, to his and his partner's understanding and communication of their needs. I took him through two of the processes I had learnt through my studies with Robbins Madanes Training (RMT): the exploring of what emotions he felt in an average week and what had to happen for him to feel that way, and the same exercise for each of the six needs.

He then explained a typical conversation he had with his partner, usually at bed time. That had me squirming in my seat because it was as though he had been sitting with a tape recorder, listening to one of my arguments with my ex.

She had come to bed rather huffily and asked him what his plans were for the next day. Noticing her huffiness but not sure what had caused it, he ignored it, replying that he was going to go fishing with Dave.

'Dave who you see every day at work? I thought as you had a free day, we could do something together.'

'Oh, I thought you had arranged to go shopping for Mum's birthday with your friends.'

'I said I might. I was waiting to see what you were doing as we haven't had a day together for weeks. We could always go shopping together.'

'Well, you may as well go shopping with your mates. You know it's not my thing, and besides, I've already told Dave.'

Seething silence.

'You just don't give a damn about me, do you?'

'Where did that come from? I only said I was going fishing.'

'This is typical of you! I'm there when you want me, but the rest of the time you don't care what I do. You always like doing things without me.'

'I'm happy in my own company, you aren't. I don't see why I should have to go shopping with you when you know I don't like it!'

'I can't talk to you when you're like this. Go to sleep!'

Lights went off and they both lay there. She was seething with hurt and pent up frustration; he was mildly confused but happy to go to sleep, assuming it would all blow over in the morning.

'We need to talk.' From her.

'What about? I don't want to talk now, I just want to go to sleep. Give us a kiss and say goodnight.'

Silence. Then the covers were roughly dragged from him and off she goes into the spare room, slamming the door behind her.

This was a typical pattern, the latest of which had led to their current off stage. When we explored how he liked to have his needs met, I asked if he had ever expressed this to his partner. Had he ever asked her the same?

The real communication behind this argument was that she was feeling devalued and unloved as a result of how distant he was. He hadn't taken on board how much notice she wanted him to take of her or how much time she wanted to spend with him. The more distant he became, the more moody and controlling she became to prod him into giving her attention.

As he was the one coming for coaching, I explained that he had the lead now in their relationship. He had the higher awareness of what was going on and what could be done differently.

What they, and indeed I, had been guilty of was not feeling brave enough to speak their truth. They were running on assumptions that the other person should simply know how they felt and respond accordingly.

It all comes down to how we view love, our model of the world and how we interpret it, and then how we transfer that to our expectations of others. If we think about what we need to feel loved, valued and certain and then give all that to our partner without stopping to consider whether that's what they need, it's no surprise that they often don't respond in kind.

In this particular case, my client asked himself how he expected his needs to be met and how reasonable they were. He then asked his partner the same questions and they were able to have an honest and open conversation that led to a deeper understanding. They are now engaged to be married.

When I caught up with him a few months later, he said, 'It's a lot easier than I thought. Not totally easy because I still can't always tell what she's thinking from what she says, but at least we can talk about it now and I can show her I love her in the way that makes sense to her, and vice versa. Not sure we will always get it right, but then no one's perfect. We can only do our best.'

Exactly.

SUMMARY & QUESTIONS

What is it people say about the word 'assume'? That it makes an ass out of you and me? How true.

When it comes to our needs and how we expect them to be met, and also noticing what is important to our significant other, we often get it wrong. This could be down to the fact that we are all self-obsessed individuals, constantly making assumptions based on our own perceptions and wondering why the pattern never seems to change. Alternatively, we may spend so long devoted to earnestly guessing what our partner wants and needs only to keep getting it wrong that we develop the belief that we must be seriously flawed in some way, incapable of ever making anyone happy, least of all ourselves.

You. How clear are you about what you really want? How do you communicate that? What is driving that? Are you assuming that others will know what you want and the ways to provide it that make you feel good just because you think it's obvious?

If we are being driven by insecurity and the need to be reassured, the way we behave might include obsessing so much about what our partner is thinking that we cannot leave them alone. We expect them to call; they don't. Our brain goes into overdrive. What are they doing or thinking? Where are they? Why haven't they done what they said they would do? Who are they with?

Enter clingy child behaviours or passive aggressive sulking. This is when we run about, finding evidence to fit either our worst fears or our confident expectations. And this is where we have to question where ownership for finding that reassurance lies.

How reasonable are you being in asking for your needs to be met? By reasonable, I mean not expecting others to second-guess you and then punishing them because they are not responding in the way you believe they should. Do you even know your needs yourself? Do you respond more to what is said to you, what you see or what you feel? Do you know the preferences of others around you?

Are you thriving on the adrenaline rush of playing games? Would you like your partner to be psychic and work out for themselves what you want, even if you keep changing the rules? Do you feel justified in punishing them if they get it wrong? How often are you punishing yourself for not getting it right? Are you taking on too much responsibility for how other people see things? Are you connecting more to others by whinging and moaning to like-minded people that your partner doesn't understand you?

Others. In relationships, the rule of thumb is how you and your partner are consistently feeling. All of the above questions can be asked to the other person in your relationship.

What effort have you made to notice or ask what your partner wants to feel loved and valued? How much attention do you pay to how they respond when they feel you are really considering them and saying or doing the things that make them feel good? Are they then more open to doing the same for you?

It's back to the focus argument again. We will find evidence to support what we choose to believe regardless of the facts. Want to think your partner is a selfish, manipulative control freak? There will be evidence aplenty! Want to believe that they, like you, are human and don't always communicate things well? You will be more likely to be tolerant and forgiving and have conversations that lead to deeper understanding and respect.

Understanding. Most people want to be understood, but one man's meat is another man's poison. Don't judge your relationship by how others seem to be in theirs. The reality is rarely what it seems.

How willing are you to understand your own needs and those of others? What difference might this understanding make to the quality of your relationships?

What if you consider the changes that you can make? Instead of assuming, ask! If what others are asking for is reasonable, even if it doesn't fit your own preferences, accept that we are all different and be willing to offer it to them. That will make for a more trusting relationship.

What is the difference between having high standards and being willing to give as well as receive and having unrealistic expectations that are impossible to meet and lead to further miscommunication? The key point is intent. If we, or others, are not made aware of the positive and negative impact of our assumptions or behaviours, then we can hardly blame ourselves, or them, for not being able to act differently. If, however, we are made aware and carry on in the same way regardless, then that becomes a choice. We then have to question how healthy the expectations are and how committed each one is to the relationship.

As my client so succinctly put it, it's not easy. But it is most definitely worth it to have a better relationship.

SEVEN

Trusting Your Instincts In A Relationship

Flowergate

'Oh, hello! You back again, Dick? Did you like the bouquet he sent you last week, hon? He is spoiling you, isn't he?'

Oh, what a priceless *Candid Camera* moment that was as I stood in a florist's shop with my then boyfriend, buying flowers to take to friends we were about to visit. I swear to God that if the ground could have opened up, 'Dick' (not his real name) would not only have dived into it but would have taken the evil incarnation of flower power woman with him.

And did the florist pause and realise the impact of her words? She did not. Fuelled by her desire for me to express my delight at the (mysterious) bouquet, she blithely carried on.

'It was a beautiful bouquet. All your favourite flowers in it,' he said, 'and the card! So thoughtful and loving.'

Through gritted teeth and sideways evils at my boyfriend, who was turning more green than the foliage he was holding, I told her that no, the flowers had not been for me.

'Are you sure? I delivered them myself.'

And there we have it. The flower lady had indeed delivered the bouquet, and this last comment prompted the boyfriend to mutter that they had been for a 'friend' and not me. As we walked away from the florist in stony silence, he assumed a nonchalant air and an increasingly familiar sneer.

'I suppose you're going to have a go at me now, aren't you?'

Oh, well done. Straight in with the critical and aggressive parent, meaning that any genuine emotional response to convey my shock and hurt was going to be dismissed as being irrational and nagging.

Amazingly, instead of taking the flowers we'd just bought and shoving them where the sun doesn't shine in absolute stroppy child mode, I stayed incredibly calm.

'I'm assuming they were for...? Could you please explain the reason why you sent them? I would like to understand why you would do that and not tell me.'

We had only been together for about five months, having met through mutual friends at a barn dance. There had been an instant physical attraction, and as it had been three years since the breakup of my last relationship, my radar at the time had been on overdrive: 'Alert! Alert! Potential new partner. All details to be filtered and distorted to suit desire to mate.' We were also rather pushed together, and when he asked me out he clearly said that he was still going through a messy divorce and had only just come out of a two-year on/off relationship with someone he had met when he first became separated. Therefore, he wasn't looking for a new relationship.

My radar at that point flashed, 'Ignore! Ignore!' as I replied, 'No problem. You are only asking me out for a drink, not to marry you.'

Long story short, we did go out and had some lovely times. However, I soon realised that he really had meant it when he said he wasn't in a good place. I found his mood swings difficult, and I reacted either as a nurturing parent or compliant child to try and second-guess his feelings in order to pep him up or appease him. I tried to build up his sense of significance by sympathising with him about his two exes, who clearly had not seen him for the wonderful man I was determined he would be, and I would be the heroine who would save him.

It was my friend Liz, the one we were on our way to visit, who pointed out how irritated I was by him within a fortnight and asked me what it was about him that made me so determined to keep going. It was in that very moment that I realised I not only had no respect for him, but I didn't even like him. Not that he was an unpleasant guy, it's just that we really didn't have anything in common. I was bored and had been desperately clinging to an ideal of being in a successful relationship, no matter what the reality.

Back to the flower shop and his response to my question.

'It was her birthday, and I as I hadn't acknowledged her at Christmas and she's going through a tough time, I thought it would cheer her up.'

On the face of it, that was fair enough as he was emulating the warm friendship that I still enjoyed with my ex. Except, this was all happening one week after I had encouraged him to meet up with her so they could have the adult conversation they hadn't had when they'd broken up. Then they could be OK to move forwards as friends, if possible. And he hadn't seen fit to tell me about the flowers.

After the meeting in question, he'd duly reported back that while it had been great to see her, she had stated clearly that she still loved him and wanted him back, so he had made it equally clear that he was now happy with me and they should wish each other well and move on.

Marvellous. I should have felt no doubt at all about his commitment then. Certainty and significance should have been abundant, along with more love and connection than you could shake a stick at. How proud I was of his growth, and of my contribution to that. The elastic of my superhero pants was positively twanging with self-congratulation.

Then came the flowers. And the fact he hadn't told me about them.

I swallowed my outrage while managing to squeak, 'OK, but I too have been going through a tough time recently, and yet I have never received any flowers. I feel you are valuing her needs over mine here.'

Meaning, 'Now listen, mate, you haven't exactly pushed the boat out in terms of making me feel sure of you, despite me constantly building your confidence and sense of self-worth by telling and showing you how important you are to me.'

'I didn't know you liked flowers.'

How I then stopped myself from jumping on his head is beyond me. In that moment, the calm adult would have said, 'You know what? It's not the flowers I'm hurt about. It's the fact that after you met with her, I specifically said that if you had stirred up any unresolved feelings and you felt you owed it to her and that relationship to try again, then that is what you must do. There is no point in us being together if you're not sure. So actually, I want to end this here and now as I realise that we are not right together. We don't meet each other's needs and this clearly isn't what either of us really want.'

Did I say that? Did I heck!

All of my uncertainty rushed to the surface, along with a maelstrom of emotions. What if I pushed him away by being stroppy? Was I being unreasonable? It was a nice thing he did, and after all, he didn't go back to her. He chose me, so why make waves?

But why did I feel so rejected and devalued? Why was I clamouring for reassurance so I could feel that all was how I wanted it to be? Because deep down, I knew it would never be so.

My superhero pants were now bunched saggily around my ankles.

The weekend, unsurprisingly, was a disaster. My inability to stuff my feelings down and accept his apology was too much in the light of all our other troubles. By trying to hang on and make more of this relationship than it was, I had pandered to my need for certainty, allowing myself to ignore his childish put downs, self-centred actions and need to prioritise only how he felt.

The fact that he would unashamedly use tears as a means to manipulate my sympathy and avoid taking on any responsibility for his own actions was becoming increasingly obvious too. This was demonstrated on the way home when I questioned him again.

'Oh, woe is me, I'm such an idiot, I don't mean to hurt anyone. I'm just struggling so much after the divorce and what it's doing to the kids. I make such a mess of things.'

My response? You guessed it: instant soothing Mummy and a renewed determination to fix this man and make him happy. All due to my unresolved need to feel needed and important by being the perfect antithesis of his previous relationships.

That lasted for two weeks until he threw a wobbly at me for wanting my dog to come up for a cuddle on the bed. After much sulking, flouncing and assertions of 'But you know my ex-wife deliberately prioritised the dogs over me, and how that made me feel', he left in the middle of the night, saying he just couldn't cope with me anymore.

He returned my belongings to me the next day. We said we would talk things over in a couple of weeks and then take it from there. We didn't. He refused to talk or meet with me, despite me writing letters and texting with childlike clinginess, and that was that.

Within a month he was back with his ex.

SUMMARY & QUESTIONS

In a nutshell, beware of what you wish for! I have used my own experience here, but it has been echoed in my work with clients, both male and female. Sometimes, when we have been on our own for a while, however happily, we get it catastrophically wrong when we feel an attraction to someone. All our values, good sense and confidence in ourselves fly out of the window as we unconsciously tap into unresolved needs and hurtle headlong into a relationship that, far from enriching us emotionally, brings us down.

And this is not always because the other person is a repeat of the 'wrong' type, as we explored in Chapter Two. We are perhaps responding more to a primal urge that it is time for us to be in a relationship again, so we get blindsided and ignore our gut instincts.

I most certainly was experienced and knowledgeable enough to recognise that, attractive as Dick was, he was no way the right man for me. His chosen lifestyle was more sedate, and he had particular issues and needs he was still working through that meant he did not have the self-confidence or strength I wanted in a partner. And I knew it. I just didn't want to admit it.

I thought I could 'fix' him to make enough changes for us to be happy and settle down. And why? Because I was lonely. I'd had enough of always being the spare wheel when out with friends and I got caught up in the initial euphoria.

You. I had to ask myself some pretty tough questions. Did the relationship end because I hadn't been understanding, accepting or giving enough? Could I have done any more? Was the reason I felt so devastated when he left because I hadn't followed my gut to end it first when Flowergate occurred? If I had followed my instinct then, could it have ended with more respect and dignity? Could we have both recognised that it wasn't working and he clearly had unresolved feelings for his ex?

I chose to carry on with the weekend and then throw myself into saving the relationship, even though I knew by that point he wasn't really what I wanted. And clearly I wasn't what he wanted either. I was being driven by my need to keep the control and certainty of the relationship, even though I knew it was dead in the water. My need for significance by proving that I was the better choice was running high, as was my need to be needed.

My sense of outrage and hurt came about because I refused to acknowledge all the warning signs. He clearly needed to be on his own to resolve his feelings and issues with his ex, but he prioritised his need to be needed because he feared being on his own. He couldn't accept the uncertainty of not having a relationship with anyone.

Which of the Transactional Analysis states was I mostly operating in? Well, adult on occasions, but if I'm honest, I mostly swung between nurturing and critical parent, which must have been very frustrating for him. In my bid to be patient and inform him of the what, how and why he was feeling, I probably came across as incredibly patronising. By being too nurturing, I was doing a good job of emasculating him by either criticising him or mummying him when he was in one of his moods. Not helpful.

Others. I may have been doing a good job of making him feel certain and loved and significant by being so available for him all the time, but I must own that my behaviours also enabled him to stay in child mode. He responded by either appeasing me, which didn't feel sincere, or being moody and stroppy, which made me even more frustrated and critical.

What was he responsible for? For not being honest – not about the flowers so much as about his real reasons for not wanting to carry on. It was easier for him, as was his pattern, to blame me for being too demanding then pick a fight over my dog, Oz, than to own the fact he wasn't happy and was confused about his feelings for his ex.

Deciding to end a relationship is always hard, especially when the old cliché 'it's not you, it's me' comes out. In my experience, if someone says that to you, then believe them. Own the fact that if you are willing to stay in a relationship when the other person is making it clear they are not committed to it, the relationship is then more about how you are choosing to meet your needs and how this is making you and your partner feel.

When we choose to be in a relationship, we also choose how we feel about it, even if it doesn't always seem that way. What if I'd just accepted that this was all Dick could offer and that being with him was better than being without him?

The yardstick for any relationship is how you consistently feel, and how you really feel about your partner. Do you really like them, or just the idea of them? If you are irritated with them within a fortnight, that is not a good sign. Choosing to ignore that will only lead to you feeling worse, not only about them but about yourself for putting up with it.

Are you feeling that you have to constantly swallow your own feelings in order not to rock the boat, only to explode at inappropriate times? Are you starting to create scripts in your head for what you wish you could say, but not saying it? Has it got to the stage that no matter what your partner says or does, you have worked yourself up into such a frenzy of annoyance and resentment they can never win?

Balance is always key. Are you doing most of the giving? Does it make you genuinely feel good? If it does, great, carry on as you are, making a conscious choice to be the giver in the relationship and expecting nothing in return. It can feel good to be the strong one. But if it doesn't feel good and you are still choosing to do it, then what impact is this having on you long term? And on others close to you?

Understanding. What did I learn from the relationship with Dick? What could I now do differently? Take more time and not rush into things, unless I'm happy to own that the attraction is only physical and the relationship may be short lived. That is perfectly fine providing both parties are honest while staying open to the possibility that the relationship may become more when they truly get to know each other.

Learn to trust your gut more. If things don't feel right, they usually aren't. If you have reached a point where your gut is hampered by your determination to be right no matter what the evidence, then it is time to look at the patterns in your relationships. Enlist someone to help you do this if necessary, especially if you are constantly asking, 'What does my partner think of me? Am I enough?'

An alternative is to ask, 'What do I think of them? Are they enough for me and what I want at this stage in my life?'

It is not about finding someone perfect, but finding someone who may be perfect for you right now. For me, Dick was perfect in helping me realise and release some of my old patterns, despite it being a painful process. Though I am now choosing to be single with the lovely Oz for company, I am far more aware of who I am and what I want, and why, which will make being honest and open in my next relationship that much easier.

And as for Dick? Well, I imagine I helped him realise what he truly wanted, which was to learn from the mistakes with his ex and try again, having seen that the grass isn't always greener. And I wish him every happiness with that.

No, really, I do! I sent flowers.

EIGHT

Calling Mr Right

When the good one goes bad

'Stop being so ridiculous. You know I love you. I shouldn't have to keep saying it.'

'Yes, I know you say you love me, so why do I feel that I'm the only one making any effort in this relationship? And do you realise you haven't touched me at all since last Tuesday? When are you going to plan something for us to do? Why are you seeing your friends again this weekend? And when are you going to the doctor about that stomach acid thing? It's really making your breath smell.'

All of this I said while sitting on the sofa at 7.30pm, enveloped in a large pink dressing gown that made me look like a furry whale. Oh, how very alluring.

This was a typical conversation with an ex who clearly fell way short of my expectations for how he should demonstrate his love for me. It didn't at the time occur to me that I was making no effort at all to show him how I loved him; I was too busy making demands and feeding my frustration at feeling unloved with a large cake and a glass of wine.

It hadn't always been that way. As in all relationships, things had started well with both of us madly besotted and desperate to show how much we loved and appreciated each other. Soon, though, familiarity crept in, along with our own ingrained beliefs about how the relationship should be and how much effort we needed to make to sustain it. Then we slid into the thoughts and behaviours that sent mixed messages to each other and resulted in a lot of confusion and negative feelings.

Tony Robbins' advice is that if we carry on doing what we did at the start of our relationship, then it would last. Sound advice, but I feel this depends on our reasons for being in the relationship in the first place and how selfish or selfless each person would deem it to be.

I have lost count of the amount of times clients have come to me with the blasé acceptance that they can never sustain the heady feelings they had at the start of their relationship, so why bother trying? It's like a foregone conclusion that love and passion won't last, which is right up there with the other cliché that you can never find all you want in one relationship, so a degree of settling for less is inevitable.

And therein lies the rub. How do we give meaning to what is selfish and selfless in our relationships when we have simply stopped trying? How can we decide that applying high standards to what we feel should happen in a relationship is sometimes unrealistic and unreasonable? How do we measure how happy we or our partners are? How do we know whether it is better to resign ourselves to this being how it will always be or walk away and find something new?

In Chapter Two, we explored how our own and others' opinions of us being with the 'wrong' person are dependent on how that person is seen to be treating us. This can also apply to being with someone who is seen to be the 'right' person. It's a kicker when people judge us for moaning about a relationship that in their eyes is 'perfect' for us.

They may even wish they had a similar relationship themselves.

'What are you moaning about? He's so reliable and kind.'

'What do you mean you're bored? He works hard all week and just wants a bit of peace and quiet when he's at home to enjoy one on one time with you.'

'I wish my partner was as considerate as yours. Mine never even notices I'm there half the time.'

'She's so lovely, like a cuddly bear.' (Oh please, let's not revisit the bear metaphor!)

And the real stinger: 'Well, of course passion doesn't last. I know she's put on a bit of weight and is a nag, but she's a great mum.' That's right up there with, 'We'd all love Brad Pitt to knock on our door and sweep us off our feet, but just be grateful your man doesn't stray like mine does.'

All these comments reflect people's own models of the world. We run our expectations of what a relationship should be by our own values and beliefs, and judge others by how we judge ourselves. Even more important is that we run these values through how we expect our needs to be met and how easy we make doing this for other people, especially when we expect them to just know. This can lead to behaviours that cause our nearest and dearest to raise their eyebrows, such as:

♡ Always moaning about our relationship yet never doing anything to put it right

♡ Always putting our partner down for not being good/sexy/exciting enough

♡ Once the initial excitement has worn off, trying to change them so they no longer resemble the person we were first attracted to

♡ No longer making any effort to be the person they were first attracted to

♡ Building up resentment and becoming obsessive over everything they say or do to prove that they are no longer 'right' for us

♡ Ending every promising relationship the minute it looks like our partner might be developing too much attachment to us.

For example, I worked with a client who had very definite beliefs about what love meant. In her eyes, if someone says they love you then they should never hurt you or lie to you because you would never do that to them. It came as a massive shock to find herself with someone who did just that. We spent a lot of time discussing that it wasn't necessarily because he didn't love her, it was simply that his paradigm for what love meant, based on his own values and beliefs, was very different to hers.

This is how we can find ourselves in a loop where we repeatedly excuse others' behaviour, blaming ourselves for being selfish and not giving enough, or punishing them for being selfish and not demonstrating the same values we hold.

This was echoed in my own experience. When I first met the person I had the longest relationship with, it was indeed, as Robbins says, a mutual frenzy of adoration. How could we make each other feel as fantastic as possible? However, within a month, the differences in our values began to appear. I continued to be the minxy, confident and sensual person I had been at the beginning, showering him with thoughtful gifts and gestures. He, though still loving and committed, became more withdrawn and didn't pay me anywhere near as much attention, which I found very confusing.

Conversations with friends to analyse this went along the lines of, 'I don't know what's wrong with him. I was wearing my most alluring outfit and being all sassy and he simply didn't come near me. Rather than throwing me down on the coach in a frenzy of desire, he now just cuddles me and puts on an episode of *Midsomer Murders*.'

'Have you talked to him about it?'

'Yes! He says that of course he still loves and desires me, but surely we don't have to keep showing it in the way we did at the beginning. That passion is not possible to maintain.'

This same conversation in various forms continued for the next two years. Was I somehow being unreasonable and unrealistic in my expectations?

When working with clients, I can easily help them identify why things appear to be going wrong in relationships, and why, as often happens, one or both partners turn to other people or circumstances to regain their sense of variety, excitement and significance. Then it becomes a case of looking at which needs are being prioritised and how they're being met.

If we've made a choice to be with someone, when is it not selfish to choose to walk away from them? Is it when their behaviour is damaging us emotionally or physically, or is it when we have an 'ideal' in our head that they don't match up to over time?

When we are not taking ownership of our needs and triggers, it becomes easy to blame the other person for letting us down. We tend to slip into the parent or child states rather than adult, as we see it, in order to try and change them and their responses.

In my case, I became highly critical and judgmental, determined to see everything my partner did as proof that he didn't love me enough. I would strop about, criticising his every gesture and condemning him as much for what he did do as what he didn't, never thinking about anything he may need to feel certain, loved and valued. It didn't occur to me that all this did was make him feel more and more emasculated and withdrawn. Like many men, he couldn't stand feeling he was not valued for who he was and that he was incapable of making his partner happy, emotionally or sexually.

I saw his increasing withdrawal from me as evidence I could present to my friends as: 'See? I told you he doesn't care!' This was further ramped up if I ever saw him being relaxed or flirty with another woman. What an insensitive and selfish traitor. I'd show him! How dare he be the person I wanted him to be with someone else and not with the shrieking, judgmental harpy I had become?

This is not to say that he didn't make his own mistakes. He would try to please and appease me, which only frustrated me further. I absolutely wanted to feel loved and respected, but I also wanted to feel he was strong and confident, someone I could rely on to understand my emotions and needs and care for me while also wanting to bend me backwards over the hostess trolley. Was that too much to ask?

Far from bringing out the best in each other, we steadily brought out the worst. Whereas he looked to his friends or hobbies to meet his needs, I increasingly looked only to him, which created even more strain as I was fast losing the confident and independent personality he had first been attracted to. In this particular case, the only thing to do was make a mutual decision to walk away, painful as the decision was.

This is what makes it hard when I coach individuals rather than couples. When a couple comes for coaching, it is fairly certain that both of them want to understand each other more and move forward in the relationship. When it is only one of them, the risk is that the other partner doesn't have the same amount of faith or commitment, so the coaching may only strengthen the individual. Sometimes, the person being coached may realise how they have been behaving and influencing the other and will change their thoughts and actions accordingly, which then has a positive impact on them both. Other times, coaching only serves to illustrate that this particular relationship is no longer salvageable, but at least the coachee can end it with dignity and authenticity, and what they've learnt will lead to a more fulfilling relationship with their next partner.

SUMMARY & QUESTIONS

Just as we may be attracted to the 'wrong' type, we may find ourselves with the 'right' type, or at least the 'right for now' type. That still presents challenges if we haven't yet mastered our own patterns of beliefs, thoughts and actions, nor our expectations of how they should be met by either ourselves or others.

Robbins has whole programmes dedicated to guiding couples to recognise their own and their partner's patterns and needs. They can then consider how to do more of what makes both partners feel good and therefore sustain the passion and commitment that was there at the beginning.

Most often, it comes back down to accepting that no one is perfect. No one person can meet all our needs all the time. The responsibility for that lies largely with ourselves as individuals.

A friend of mine illustrated this recently with an anecdote from her own relationship. She has been with her partner happily for over ten years, both having had long term relationships before, and she freely admits that he is vastly different from her other partners. He is steady and analytical and not given to being overly emotional, and the much younger her would not have been interested in him as he would not have met her need for variety and significance.

Throughout the years, they have had, like all couples, their ups and downs, mostly concerning the huge difference in how they each express their love and commitment. Both are very independent but supportive of each other's careers, and they share a lot of fun and laughter together. She is open, affectionate and extremely considerate of other people's needs and feelings. He is far more self-contained and has a genuine belief that it is not selfish to accept what others want to do or give to him as they are making the choice to do so. This does not mean he doesn't appreciate or reciprocate, but he doesn't necessarily show that in the way she would like.

For example, she would love to express more vulnerability and lean on him for emotional support. However, this triggers unpleasant associations with his ex, resulting in him shutting down, calling her over-emotional and telling her to 'get a grip'. At first, she felt hugely hurt and rejected by this and considered leaving him to look for a different relationship. This was compounded by their different coping mechanisms: her discomfort at any confrontation and his passive aggressive sulking rather than admitting his feelings or saying sorry.

Being an extremely talented coach, she learnt to accept that she would always have the upper hand in being able to broker peace by 'managing' how she communicated her needs and adjusting her expectations of him. And why? Because she recognised that she could. She concluded that there was so much of the relationship that she did value, it was OK to accept that their different style of loving and communicating was something she was prepared to live with.

When I explain this concept to clients, I often get an outraged response of, 'Well, that's just dishonest manipulation.'

Is it? Or is it accepting that we are all different and that we 'manage' each other according to how we choose to respond and what we choose to prioritise. The acceptance level for that is going to be different for every couple. In my friend and her partner's case, they have a strong bond, an unshakeable belief that they are each loved and an enjoyment and acceptance of their differences. This meets their core needs for certainty, variety, significance and love and connection.

You. What makes the relationship right? What is enough? On a day to day basis, how loved, accepted and connected do you feel? Do you love your partner enough to be the one who understands, manages or gives more? Do you know that your partner will step up and do the same for you only not necessarily in the same way?

Or is it always one sided? Do you feel they are taking you for granted? Are *you* taking you for granted because you haven't got the courage to explain your needs and how to get them? Do you understand what your partner needs in return?

At what point do you perhaps stop recognising and allowing the different ways you each express love or not taking the time to keep communication open? Does this lead to situations where you look elsewhere for validation, love and connection that may ultimately have a negative impact on your relationship?

Others. What first attracted you to the relationship? How long term do you want it to be? It is perfectly OK to connect with someone because of where you are and what needs you want to meet at the time, providing you are not behaving in a way that is disrespectful or damaging to your partner?

How much of their behaviour is really the issue? If you genuinely feel the changes in them are more to do with their own issues no matter what you do, then it is not selfish, in my opinion, to walk away.

As my gorgeous friend Beth says, 'The best relationships are the ones where we strengthen ourselves as individuals first.' Learning to consistently apply the thoughts and actions that make us feel self-love and confidence give us more tolerance for our partner. Deciding to be loving and giving in the face of our differences is not being weak; it is demonstrating an authentic sense of who we really are, and then the choice becomes how long we want to hold that for that person. No one else has the right to judge. It is our decision to stay or leave, but at least we will make it with the best intention of being true to ourselves and allowing our partner to do the same.

Understanding. The key question is what is OK for you?

What rules and beliefs are driving you? What type of person triggers your reactions? What control can you choose to take over how you respond?

Accepting our differences may mean that however unintentionally we may have hurt others and however contrite and determined we may be to make amends, we may not always get resolution or a happy ending. We can never control what others are willing to accept and forgive, only what we choose to accept. Sometimes relationships are strengthened by tough times and acceptance of mistakes as growth for the individual and as a relationship, sometimes they're not. The 'right' relationship may only be 'right' for the lessons it teaches us which, though sometimes painful to accept, is all part of having the ability to make different choices next time.

I have learnt to understand that perfection doesn't exist, but sometimes it is about looking at the picture as a whole.. and Now I am clearer on accepting myself and what really makes me feel happy, I am far more willing to stop looking for 'perfection' in others. There are a lot of different people out there who can meet our needs in lots of different ways.

Question is, what is your smorgasbord of potential partners going to look like? How often are you going to keep choosing the same things to go on it? What might it be like if you changed that? Love doesn't always have to last forever to be of value.

NINE

When Our Most Important Relationship Is With Our Pet

'You do realise that your most significant relationship is with a dog? And that is *so* not normal.'

Well, first of all, if there is no such thing as a perfect relationship, then there most certainly is no such thing as a 'normal' one. The above quote, which has often been said to me, evokes a response of, 'Absolutely! You find me a man who will love me unconditionally, meet all my needs for security, variety, significance, connection, growth and contribution and never, ever judge me, then we'll start talking about normal.'

The whole point of being in any kind of relationship is to have our needs met in positive ways that make us feel fulfilled and happy. Most especially, this includes the relationship we have with ourselves. And yes, while I am happy to be single and a doting owner to Oscar, my golden Labrador, I am aware that this relationship involves some pretty good avoidance tactics in terms of wanting to share my life with a man. Not that the two relationships are mutually exclusive.

I have always been happy to own that as my choice, but recently, some questions asked of me at the Strategic Intervention Coaching caused me to stop and consider how exactly I was meeting my needs for a fulfilling relationship. What impact was Oscar having on that both positively and negatively?

Comments such as, 'It is great that you are such a loving person, but are you using Oz as an excuse not to be open to sharing your life with someone?' made me think. Not at first, of course. My initial reaction was to go into defensive denial, which in itself gave me insight that this was something I hadn't been prepared to consider.

I stepped back and further considered the fact that we become defensive when someone questions our choices, particularly if the question is asked from what we perceive to be a judgmental standpoint. Is it any different if someone questions our relationship with a pet as opposed to a human partner? The automatic reaction is to assume we are being judged as strange for being so devoted to a pet and choosing to be single. Yet, is that any different to the judgement we place on another person's choice of partner?

'I can't believe he/she stays with them when they treat her/him so badly.'

'He's playing away again. I think she knows but doesn't want to admit it.'

'He's always putting her down in public and blowing hot and cold. She doesn't ever know where she stands.'

'She never looks happy. She complains a lot but she won't do anything about it.'

'Do you see how she is all over his friends but is very cold with him?'

'He/she is more devoted to the dog than to his/her partner. It's not normal.'

All critical parent mode questions with the implication that if we were that person, we would never behave in such a way. Nor would we allow ourselves to be treated in such a fashion. Oh, really?

Well, I never have to think or say anything like that about Oscar.

Just as people become defensive if someone criticises their partner or their choice to be with that person, the same thing happens when someone criticises my dog. And I absolutely know I'm not alone. Comments from friends, acquaintances or complete strangers such as: 'He's very dependent on you, isn't he?'; 'He sleeps on the bed with you? No wonder you're single!'; 'I bet he takes a lot of feeding as he obviously likes his food'; 'I used to have a fat dog like that, but he died'; 'Oh, you really love him, don't you? You are going to be devastated when he dies,' could also be said of a human partner. And the mix of critical and nurturing parent states above would evoke a similar response from me. My natural instinct would be to go into full stroppy, rebellious child mode.

'Oh really? Have you looked in the mirror lately, you fat gimp? Yes, he does love his food, and I work very hard to balance what he eats against the amount of exercise he can do because of his arthritis, you moron. Yes, I will be completely devastated when he dies, which is not going to be until he is at least fifty-two in human years.'

I will admit, sometimes I do occasionally respond like that, but mostly I try to be adult and walk away, muttering to Oz and cuddling up to him even more when we get home to the sofa. Much as anyone who has ever felt the need to defend their human partner would do.

And now we get to taking ownership of the needs.

Oscar came into my life for the last two years of my relationship with 'Romeo' (not his real name, but his *nom de plume*). We had been together for four years and it is fair to say that all was not well. We loved each other, but we were not consistently meeting enough of each other's needs for a fulfilling relationship. At the time, I was travelling each month to Oxford as part of my coaching training and passed by a rescue puppy centre. Not going in was torture. Although I had promised Romeo I would never push to get a dog even though I was desperate for one, of course, I went in.

The centre was shutting down that day and there were three puppies left: a golden Lab, a white Samoyed and a

Rottweiler. All three were utterly gorgeous, but the Rottweiler was staying with the family that ran the centre and a couple was coming back to check out the Samoyed again. This left the four-month-old wonky pawed, overweight golden blob who rolled onto his back with a facial expression that would have melted even the most hardened non-pet-lover. Immediately, my nurturing Mama genes came into play and I rang Romeo, begging him to be OK with me bringing him home.

It's not hard to guess what needs were being met here. My need to gain significance and love and connection overrode Romeo's hesitation, and while he did indeed fall in love with Oscar, my complete disregard for his opinion started us down a slippery slope.

Romeo, though incredibly creative and artistic, prioritised certainty and liked to remain in control of his environment and routine, even though that routine may have been very varied. He didn't want to have this disrupted, or develop a love connection with something that would add to that disruption. And he never quite forgave me for this.

Like many couples who get a pet to fill a gap, we officially made Oscar Prince Fur Face in terms of the love and devotion we poured on to him. He became our substitute for connecting with each other. All our conversations now centred on him and his needs, and the divide between us became wider as a result.

For the next two years, rather than focusing on Romeo, I gained my certainty from ensuring Oscar's routine and care were prioritised. I got lots of variety because I was out and about with him, meeting other dog owners. Love and connection came from Oscar and I felt hugely significant because I was his chief carer, responsible for all his needs. I also felt a sense of contribution to the welfare of others, growing through learning about taking care of a dog with special health needs. In return, he loved me unconditionally.

And what of Romeo? Well, we had an increased shared connection with Oscar, but other than that, we simply stopped looking for ways to make each other feel certain, valued or loved in any significant way, growing further apart. Neither of us deliberately set out to hurt the other, but as the cracks in our relationship deepened, we became less and less adult with each other. Instead, our conversations became increasingly judgemental, especially from my side as I poured all my frustration and loneliness into criticising him for not being as vigilant with Oscar's needs as I was. I turned Oscar into something else to make him feel bad about.

Tony Robbins explains in great detail the need to keep doing what we did at the beginning of a relationship as that is what will keep us together. With Romeo and me, all the tolerance, care, infatuation, thinking of the other first and finding new ways to keep the spark lit fell away. We drifted into a mundane routine, forgetting all the things about the other person that made us fall in love in the first place. Of course, we couldn't *make* each other feel unhappy, but our behaviours certainly influenced it.

In summary, there is absolutely nothing wrong with developing a strong bond with a pet, nor in choosing to be single after a relationship breaks down. I often work with clients who are desperate to maintain a link with their ex and remain friends, and often a pet can be just as much a bridge as a child. But a friendship cannot exist between exes without the buffer of time so that all the hurt and disappointment of the relationship break-up can settle, allowing for the re-establishment of trust in order to move forwards.

People often assume that it is a significant concrete betrayal that erodes trust within a relationship, but in my experience, both personally and professionally, it is never that simple. The biggest erosion of trust comes from the gradual introduction of behaviours and responses that leave one or both in the relationship feeling consistently not as important to the other person as they once were. It is often hard to put our finger on it, and trying to communicate it can lead to a criticism of being 'over-emotional' or 'paranoid'. However, it is very real, and it is no wonder that we then look for other ways to meet our need for significance and certainty.

SUMMARY & QUESTIONS

You. Why did I choose to put my dog over my relationship? If I had known then what I know now, would things have been different? Possibly, but who knows?

I was not the person then that I am now. I didn't have the knowledge, self-awareness or skills to identify what patterns of thinking and behaving I was stuck in. Based on my insecurities rather than my worth, I fixated on getting the love and attention I thought I deserved, punishing Romeo for not being everything I felt he 'should' be. I also punished myself for not being enough for him.

Oscar was the source of unconditional love I was yearning for. Having not had children, I had a need to nurture and care for a dependent, which he fulfilled. He gave me a real sense of connection and significance, and I had absolute certainty that he loved me, no matter what. It was far easier to focus on maintaining that than face the fact I was running away from looking at how I was responsible for the breakdown of my relationship. It was far easier to blame Romeo for not giving me what I needed than take ownership for myself.

Free Discovery Session
with Rebecca Miller!

This voucher entitles you to one 60 Minute Discovery Session with proof of purchase of my book, Start With You!

To redeem your voucher, please contact me on 07931554462 or at **hello@beccymiller.com** or here at Lifehouse, quoting '*Start With You*'.

I look forward to hearing from you!

Others. Does the above sound at all familiar? We often look to others to give us what we feel is missing in our key relationship, and justify it by looking for evidence to validate the belief that our partner isn't good enough or doesn't love us enough to give us what we want.

How may others be feeling as a result to us devoting such a huge amount of time and attention to a pet? What impact does this have on their needs being met?

We put all the emphasis on making them responsible for how we feel, and so either develop behaviours that push them further away or become an insecure mess with yet more reason to cry, 'See, no one will ever love me enough. At least with my children/pet, I know I am loved.'

Well, absolutely with children, but not for as long as we think because the pesky little blighters are also complex individuals who insist on having their needs met. So really, a pet is your best bet. And a wonderful excuse not to focus on being responsible for your own well-being or developing the skills to give to someone else in a mutually rewarding relationship.

How were my behaviours and responses impacting on others? How much attention did I pay to Romeo's needs or feelings? In my determination to be both 'the fixer' of the relationship and 'the victim' in terms of not feeling valued enough, how much was I considering my own responsibility? How much was I considering the rejection he may have felt?

Understanding. We can never go back in time, no matter how much we want to. Torturing ourselves about what could have been is a one-way ticket to constant heartache, shutting off our ability to grow from the experience and move on to something different, if not better.

At the end of the day, loving and caring for a beloved pet is a sure-fire way to fulfil our needs, and is also a proven way of calming us down and relieving the effects of stress and trauma. However, this may stop us from finding other means to meet those needs. How much anxiety was I still including in my life to prioritise my pet at the expense of my own self-care and willingness to connect with others in the same way? How much was I using him as an excuse not to address my real issue of being too fearful to put myself out there and explore meeting my needs with an actual partner?

Also, how was I considering Oscar's needs? By over-humanising him, was I not providing what he needed as a dog? As in a relationship with another human, a pet's needs count too. We can't just use them to meet our needs to the detriment of their well-being. And unlike a human, an animal can't voice this.

The understanding I have taken from this is that it is absolutely fine to choose to be single, and also to choose to meet all your emotional needs through your pet. However, own the fact that this relationship is not perfect, and that it may be an excuse not to deal with your personal issues and how these affect your relationships with others.

Oscar is helping me take ownership of my decisions and choices in how I relate to others and how I am choosing to meet my needs. My ongoing lesson is to keep aware of which needs I am prioritising and how I give and receive love. Then I can more easily shift this to come from a place of self-worth rather than insecurity. And this learning will be Oz's biggest gift to me when this relationship too eventually comes to an end.

TEN

Six Needs And Getting The Right Ingredients

How to be OK with creating relationships that are perfectly flawed

'You realise that you will find it very difficult to meet a man who's right for you?'

'What makes you say that?'

'Well, you are beautiful, intelligent, strong, independent, confident, empathetic and talented. It will take a strong man to be OK with all of that.'

This was a comment made to me by a male friend a year ago. While I now thank him for the kind words, they very briefly flung me into a pit of despair. A rush of old values

163

and limiting beliefs from the ghosts of relationships past rose up in glee, whooping with delight.

'Yes! Tear up the P45, we're back in business. We knew this newfound wisdom and progress not perfection rubbish would crumble in the end.'

Well, sorry to disappoint you, lads. While I appreciate that you may still visit occasionally, your role is now that of consultant only.

Throughout this book, I have tried to give some context to recognising our needs and the patterns of beliefs and actions we have developed within our relationships to meet them. This recognition will always remain a work in progress, so we may have those voices from the past rattling around. In fact, that is a good thing because they serve an important purpose.

Those voices and the lapses into old patterns remind us that we are human and we will never get it right all of the time. And neither will anyone else. While I would have made an excellent beauty pageant speech by wanting universal love and world peace, which I absolutely do, wouldn't life then be that little bit more dull and predictable?

Without contrast and reminders of the mistakes we make and the lessons we learn, we would never feel the need to dream and grow and stretch ourselves to be more and feel more than we currently do. Then we would miss out on having relationships that make us stronger and happier because we would have missed out on the importance of starting with ourselves.

To quote Abraham Hicks, 'Nothing is more important than that you feel good.'

This doesn't mean running amok with other people's lives and feelings, but taking care of how you feel about yourself first. As these chapters will have demonstrated, we can only make better choices for ourselves and our relationships from a place of feeling good, using whatever means feel right for us as individuals. Choice and awareness of intent are everything.

So, rather than believe my friend and accept his doom and gloom prediction about my future, I responded with that age-old mysterious question, 'And?'

Last I checked, I didn't need a romantic partner as one of my chief needs for survival. It's just that having one, if it feels right, makes the journey a lot more interesting and fun. The metaphor I use with myself and my clients to illustrate this is a cake.

A cake can be delicious on its own. Having icing on it adds another layer of deliciousness and flavour, but it is an extra. It isn't essential to the cake. No one has a go at you for taking the icing off the Christmas cake if that is not your thing, yet some feel they have the right to question your choice whether to remove a partner from your life and go it alone.

The key question is what are you happy to settle for? I don't mean settle as in accepting second best, but what is realistic for you if you are happy to accept that nothing and no one is perfect? What ingredients are right for you and how might they be adapted or change?

This makes it easier to answer the following questions.

Are you choosing to be alone because you fear you will never find someone good enough? Do you believe that no one will love you for who you are, flaws and all, even though others may describe those flaws as strengths?

Are you choosing to be in a relationship because you are too scared to be alone? Is the option of taking ownership of what you truly want from a relationship to make you feel more fulfilled too scary and unknown?

Are you avoiding having any kind of 'icing' because experience has taught you it isn't good for you? Are you determined to stick to one type of cake? Are you choosing to be alone because, actually, that's how you prefer it, but you reserve the right to change your mind if you meet someone who looks like they could be the icing on your cake? Or are you still stuck on feeling you have to be perfect to deserve love, and so does the person/relationship you choose to be in?

The choice is yours. As a coach, I never impose my personal beliefs on to my clients, but I do get them to ask themselves questions like the ones above. This makes them stop, think and make a decision that they are happy to own, even if it doesn't lead to what I or anyone else would want for them. My job is to create that space for them so they can raise their understanding and awareness of their fundamental beliefs, values and needs. They then use the appropriate tools and strategies to take ownership of their choices, and be open to making different ones should they want to.

If I had to sum up all I have learnt, both personally and through the wonderful clients I have had the privilege to work with, I would apply the six human needs to my own life as follows:

Certainty. To have certainty, do I have to be absolutely sure of everything all of the time? Am I in danger of creating so many rules in order to feel safe, that I never feel happy with how things are? How could they be if I chose to take ownership of what is in my control rather than stressing about what isn't? What would living and loving a little less fearlessly really look like?

If I look at the smorgasbord of options around me and rely on my own experiences and insight, I will have a better chance of choosing the people I know make me feel good about myself. If I then choose to pick someone from the naughty table, even though experience tells me they certainly won't be good for me, I can own that too and the consequences it may bring, both good and bad and then choose what to do differently if I want to.

I am also certain that the more I start with myself, the more likely I am to attract the kind of partner my friend thinks will be so difficult. Knowing myself, all of myself including the messy bits, is key and reducing the rules that I make around being perfect will make it easier for me to accept that it is all about the progress, not the achievement.

Variety/uncertainty. It is great to have variety in life and to push the boundaries of how much uncertainty I am prepared to handle in my relationships, providing it feels good for the majority of the time. It's all about the balance. Am I in danger of not having enough variety in my life because I am scared to take risks and allow for the differences that make us all unique? Or am I hooked on either creating or getting involved in drama because I fear being bored? Am I too scared to face up to things I need to take ownership of and so choose the wrong types? Am I allowing my own sense of self-worth and well-being to suffer by basing all of my responses on how someone else is behaving instead of taking ownership of my own behaviour? Yes, I will continue to make mistakes, the point is what I choose to do about them and how I develop my ability to express my needs in ways that they are more likely to be met, even if that may be in ways I've not experienced before.

Significance. No one on this planet will love you unconditionally unless they have fur and four legs. Or feathers and two legs. And even then you may be pushing it.

The most important person I need to feel valued by is me. Then I can look for ways to feel further valued by the people I choose to be with, so long as I don't expect all my feelings of significance to come from them. They will not be able to read my mind, however much I stare at them. Successful relationships take communication and flexibility and the mindfulness that we are not the centre of the universe, just our own. No one judges us as harshly as we do ourselves and recognising the triggers for when we feel devalued and why needs to start with us. Accepting that it is perfectly ok to be selfish and take care of our own needs first is essential because, as the saying goes, you can't give to others from an empty tank. Prioritising ourselves from a sense of love and compassion and the intent to give without damaging ourselves is very different from continuing patterns of behaviour that place unreasonable demands on ourselves or others. And it is OK if someone prefers to be with someone else other than me because that is all part of the learning.

Love and connection. Connection comes in all shapes and sizes. I can choose to connect with others to make me feel good, or to continue to make me feel bad. The expression of like attracts like is very true.

Owning what the connection is really about in terms of what needs I am meeting goes a long way to helping me stop blaming myself and others for not always getting it right. Also, not all connections have to be long term. There is sometimes more power in the brief moments I spend with someone than with a lifelong commitment.

The more aware I am of the intent behind the connection and what it is giving me, the more control I can choose to have over my expectations and what I am prepared to give.

Growth. We cannot help but grow through our encounters with other people, events and circumstances. How much we grow is a personal choice and a matter of attitude.

I can choose to sit on my stump and ignore the lessons each relationship brings me, continuing to make the same mistakes or have the same unrealistic expectations, or I can learn to be more adaptable. If I stop blaming myself and others for mistakes and instead look for the patterns I am creating, I can then choose to do things differently next time.

We are not alone – there is a lot of support out there if we choose to access it.

Contribution. This is where I need to take ownership of the fact that if I pause long enough and look around to see how I can contribute to things and people outside myself, the rest of my needs will all fall into place. Then they will be met very easily.

I'm not advocating morphing into Mother Teresa, Gandhi or the Dalai Lama; I am saying that when I stop obsessing about myself, life does generally look a lot better. Yes, I need to start with myself, as we all do, and learning and growing to help with that is the theme of this book. However, becoming so self-obsessed that I forget to take ownership of the effect of what I do on others can lead me further away from creating fulfilling relationships, not closer.

Contributing by being more generous with my willingness to forgive is a good place to start, acknowledging that we all make mistakes. How I choose to feel and what I choose to do in response to others can make a huge impact not only on myself, but also them. It's not always easy. I know only too well how painful and dark it can be when I feel so low

I question what I can possibly contribute to anyone. But I also know how quickly that can shift when I focus on the little things that show me that I do make a difference, and that is something I can choose to nourish.

So there you have it: my personal method for happily accepting that the recipe I choose to follow will be forever adapted and tweaked as I continue my own *Bake Off* journey and add the ingredients of the people I share my life with, both professionally and personally. My hope is that you will have found this book useful in helping you do the same.

In the Resources section I have continued the theme of *Start With You* by providing information that I have personally found useful in my own life and coaching. Choose to take whatever is relevant to your own intent to take ownership of yourself and create different ways of feeling and behaving in your relationships.

Just before I finish, I'd like to return briefly to the cake metaphor. My special cake for my friend Judith and her family is what she lovingly refers to as 'chocolate road kill cake'. This is due to the cake never surviving the car or bike journey to her house very well, arriving looking like it has indeed been in a road traffic accident. However, it always tastes good, and I have never felt I had to change anything in it as Judith and her family love it, and me for making it, just as it is. And that to me is perfect.

I wish you every success and hope you get creative with what you choose to add or remove from your own recipe for how you want to be. What different flavours are out there you haven't tried yet? We are all works in progress, so own who you are, get clear on what you like and don't like, what you want and don't want, and why. All cake, when mixed and baked properly, is good cake, no matter how plain or fancy. People's opinions of that cake are just that: opinions, not fact. So the best opinion to start with is the one you have of yourself, I wish you every success!

Resources

Human Needs Psychology

Websites

To find out more about Tony Robbins, the theories and practice behind Human Needs Psychology, and his partner, Cloe Madanes, please go to:

www.rmtcenter.com

www.tonyrobbins.com

Both www.rmtcenter.com and www.strategicintervention.com hold registers of their certified practitioners, of which I am one.

For a more visual introduction, head over to www.ted.com, the site for 15-minute inspirational talks given by experts in their field. Tony Robbins has one called, 'Why we do what we do?'

Books

Awaken the Giant Within, Tony Robbins, Simon and
Schuster 1991

Unlimited Power: The New Science of Personal Achievement,
Tony Robbins, Simon and Schuster 1997

Relationship Breakthrough, Cloe Madanes, New York Rodale
2009

The Strategic Intervention Handbook, Magali and Mark
Peysha, Strategic Intervention Press 2014

The Relationship Cure: A 5 Step Guide To Strengthening
Your Marriage, Family And Friendships, John M Gottman,
Random House New York 2001

Transactional Analysis

TA is a theory developed from the work of Dr Eric Berne.
A popular and easy introduction to this is in his own
book, *The Games People Play*, published by Penguin Life. A
more in depth analysis and application of his theories can
be found in his book, *Transactional Analysis in Psychotherapy*,
published by Souvenir Press.

Thomas A Harris, psychiatrist, associate and friend of Eric Berne, wrote *I'm OK, You're OK*, published by Arrow Press.

An in depth study and evaluation of the TA theory and how it has evolved is *TA Today* by Ian Stewart and Vann Joines, Lifespace Publishers.

Neuro-linguistic Programming

NLP, devised by Richard Bandler and John Grinder in the 1970s, is based on the premise that we experience the world through our senses and translate this into our thought processes, both conscious and unconscious. These then influence and affect our physiology, emotions and behaviour. NLP helps show you how to recode your experiences and alter your internal programming to get different results.

Websites
www.nlpinfo.com

Books
Frogs into Princes, RIchard Bandler and John Grinder, Eden Grove Editions, Revised edition June 1990

Neuro-Linguistic Programming for Dummies, Romilla Ready and Kate Burton, John Wiley and Sons Ltd, revised edition October 2015

EFT: Emotional Freedom Technique or 'Tapping'

Emotional Freedom Techniques is a self-help method based the work of Gary Craig in the 1990s. EFT uses elements of Cognitive Therapy and Exposure Therapy, and combines them with Acupressure in the form of fingertip tapping on twelve acupuncture points. There is an increasing body of medical evidence and research papers that support how effective EFT is for phobias, anxiety, depression, posttraumatic stress disorder, pain and other problems.

By uncovering and acknowledging the true emotions and feelings linked to specific memories or beliefs, it is easier to change the focus and language we use and helps clear the way for more empowering beliefs and actions.

Websites
Further information and a 60-page free download of the essentials of EFT can be found at www.EFTuniverse.com

Other resources and information can be found at
www.thetappingsolution.com or at
Penny Croal's www.changeaheadbiz.com
Sarah Ridout at www.positivelifezone.com

Other useful websites

www.abrahamhicks.com the originator of law of
attraction that precedes *The Secret*
www.louisehay.com
www.sprinkleofgreen.com
www.thefashionfoodie.com
www.fitcetera.co.uk
www.lifehouse.co.uk
www.daringandmighty.com
www.hendriks.com

Books

Ask and it is Given: Learning to Manifest the Law of Attraction – Learning to Manifest Your Desires, Esther Hicks, Hay House Publishing 2010

Daring Greatly: How the Courage to Be Vulnerable Transforms the Way We Live, Love, Parent and Lead, Brene Brown, Penguin Life 2015

Don't Let Anything Dull Your Sparkle, How to Break Free from Negativity and Drama, Doreen Virtue, Hay House UK 2015

Love For No Reason, 7 Steps for Creating a Life of Unconditional Love, Marci Shimoff, Simon and Schuster 2011

Happiness For No Reason, 7 Steps to Being Happy from the Inside Out, Marci Shimoff and Carol Kline, Simon and Schuster 2008

Conscious Loving: Gay and Kathlyn Hendricks, Bantam Books 1992

Acknowledgements

To Mikey, who inspired me to write this, many thanks.

I would like to thank Joe, Lucy and Alison at Rethink Press for allowing me to even get started on this book. I am very grateful for their enthusiasm, support and much appreciated constructive criticism.

Thanks to all my wonderful clients, who have all helped me learn and grow. Special thanks to Sophie Adams, Claire Riddell and Shirley Cooper.

Huge thanks to all at RMT and the Strategic Intervention Institute; your training and support has made such a difference to me both professionally and personally. Special thanks to Mark and Magali Peysha, Beth Wolfe, Jeremy Fuhs, Bangorn Foster, Nicole Gruel and my good pal Simon Kanani for all the talks, learning, laughs and inspiration.

For my brother Steve, who has been on an incredible journey and of whom I am so proud. Love and gratitude also to our parents who taught us so much, no longer with us but forever in our hearts.

To Sue Davis at Lifehouse Spa and Hotel, who gave me the opportunity to coach there and be part of a fantastic team, thank you.

Last, but not least, thanks to my wonderful pals who have endured me writing, procrastinating, falling off the edge of the planet at times for helping me in all ways emotional and physical. Lisa, Ellie, Liz, Hannah, Tingles, Rosie, Tracey, and Paul – where would I be without you?

Special thanks to Roz Birch for her enthusiasm, support, input and feedback; Bonnie Friend for her encouragement and wisdom; and Vicky May, my friend, confidante, prosecco partner, supporter and substitute family. Thank you so much.

The Author

Rebecca began her career as a teacher and still works in education as a consultant and trainer for Osiris Educational. She specialises in working both with senior leaders and with teachers on the ground to improvie children's engagement with learning. Her passion for developing Growth Mindset and a coaching approach to creating positive results dovetails with her own coaching practice and can be found in her previous book, *Clearly Outstanding*.

While teaching, Rebecca began studying for her Masters in Coaching and Mentoring at Oxford Brookes University. Since then she has trained and gained further coaching qualifications with the Robbins Madanes Institute and Institute for Strategic Intervention. She specialises in applying the key skills and strategies to coach individuals in any area of their life, but particularly enjoys working with couples as part of her training in divorce prevention, and with individuals struggling with relationships.

As well as coaching privately, Rebecca works as a coach for Lifehouse Spa and Hotel in Thorpe-le-Soken, Essex and writes a regular blog for them.

Rebecca currently lives in North Essex with her dog, Oscar.

To learn more about Rebecca and her coaching, go to her website, www.oscarresourcecoaching.com

Lightning Source UK Ltd.
Milton Keynes UK
UKOW05f1156060317
295907UK00007B/59/P